AND INSTRUCTIVE STORY

THE SIMPLE TALE
OF
SUZAN AKED
OR
*INNOCENCE AWAKENED
IGNORANCE DISPELLED*

HONNI SOIT QUI MAL Y PENSE

PRINTED FOR
THE EROTICA BIBLION SOCIETY
OF
LONDON AND NEW-YORK
1898

THE SIMPLE TALE

OF

SUSAN AKED

CHAPTER I

GENESIS

We used to live at the foot of the continuation of the range of the Malvern Hills, on the borders of Herefordshire and Worcestershire. That is, my father, mother, I, and an old faithful servant, Martha Warmart, who were inseparable. Martha had been my mother's maid before she married my father, and was quite a confidential member of the family. Indeed, the idea of her leaving us never entered either her head or that of any of us. Our other servants rarely stayed longer than a year or so, because we lived in such a quiet humdrum spot and amongst such perfect clodhoppers, that there was a scarcity of beaux; and what woman, saving a staid elderly one, can be expected to like a place where the engaging male sex is so sadly wanting?

Until I was sixteen years old I had lived in this dear old house, and so even and tranquil was my life that I never contemplated leaving it. If my father and mother had grown any older during those years I did not notice it. To me they were ever the same, and so indeed was Martha. My father was a great reader of books, much versed in science, and his delight and my pleasure was my being taught by him. Botany, geology, animal and insect nature formed the chief and most interesting portion of our studies; but history, geography, French and Italian also found their place. I learnt to play the piano from my mother, and altogether, though completely without society, my education would have done me credit had I had the advantages of a town maiden's life. As I have said before I was as happy as the day was long, never knowing what a violent emotion was like.

But all this was to come now to an end. One fine morning in the early summer, oh! I have cause to remember the 6th of June! my mother came down to breakfast without my father. She told me she supposed it was a long walk he had taken with me the day previous which must have tried him, but that he was so sound asleep she had not the heart to waken him. We ate our breakfast as usual, only taking care to make as little clatter as possible with our knives, forks, cups and spoons, lest any little clink, clink, might reach the ears of the dear sleeper above, and waken him from a sound and refreshing sleep. Ah! me!

I went out into the garden to see what new flowers had blossomed into beauty, and to pick a nice posy for my father, who loved flowers, when I heard my mother shrieking out for Martha. The tone of her voice alarmed me, and I flew to see what was amiss. My mother, seeing me rushing upstairs, called louder still for Martha, who, with the servants as alarmed as myself, came running as fast as such an ancient body could, all with faces full of consternation. My poor mother, seeing us all coming, went into her bedroom, and, pointing to my father, said ; " I don't know what is the matter with him; but I cannot wake him! " I ran forward, but Martha pushed me on one side, saying, " Not yet, miss Susan dear! " and went and gazed earnestly in my father's face. He was lying on one side in the position of a person sound asleep.

Oh! he was dead! dead! He had died probably very early in the morning, for he was quite cold and stiff : he must have been dead hours. The agony of the discovery was unbearable. It was such a dreadful, dreadful shock! but what followed intensified our grief and horror, and made it seem as though all the miseries man was capable of enduring were being showered down upon our devoted heads. My darling mother never spoke again! She sank into a chair, gasped once or twice, and before anyone could run to her help, she fell to the floor, literally heart-broken. I must beg permission to cease from any further details of the most excruciatingly agonizing moments I ever spent. I do not even remember how the hours, the days, and the weary nights passed. I was stunned with the overwhelming grief and desolation that came upon me, and I can only liken myself to a happy bird, a native of the tropics, suddenly moved from its joyous surroundings to an Arctic desert.

The first distinct thing I can remember was old Martha telling me I should write to my father's man of business, old Penwick, whom I had seen several times when he came to see my poor dear father on business. I did so. Worcester where he resided, was not very distant from us, but news from our part of the world travelled slowly along the country roads, and my letter reached Mr. Penwick before rumour. The old gentleman was inexpressibly shocked and grieved. I find that suddenness has a great deal to do with feelings of that kind— not that I think Mr. Penwick would have shown less sympathy had my parents died after a long illness instead of in the sudden manner they did; but the blow, coming like a thunderclap as it happened, certainly caused him intense pain, and made his benevolent old heart open towards me in a most tender and fatherly manner. He advised me to think of some of my nearer relations, and to write and ask some one of them to come and stay with me awhile, until some plan for the future could be made, for there would be some work for the lawyers, and much to be done before my affairs could be put into good order. I was a minor, too, and must have a guardian.

My father's will had to be discovered, and whilst all this was being done, as my presence was necessary, Mr. Penwick said I ought to have some one to stay and live with me, to cheer me up and divert my unhappy thoughts into some brighter and altogether different channel. I felt too languid, too indifferent. My simple prayers were that I too might die, and go to that happy land where I had been taught to believe my loved parents had gone, and where I might be with them for ever -

Had my cousins the Althairs been still at Leigh, Mr. Penwick would have called on his way in and out from Worcester, and asked my aunt to let one of the girls come to keep me company; but they had gone to live in France. There were other less well-known cousins of mine, one of whom my mother had invited to make short stays with me some six years back. I did not care much for her, as she was a town girl, with ideas and pursuits altogether different from mine, and I remembered being offended with her for sneering, as I thought, at my " beetle and pebble hunting " occupations, which to her were tiresome and uninteresting. Somehow her name came into my head—Lucia Lovete—and it was to her that Mr. Penwick wrote. Lucia had lost her parents when very young; like myself, she was an only child, and she lived at Sunninghill with another cousin a little older than herself, Gladys Spendwell. In my heart I thought Lucia would never care to come, and I really hoped she would not. I was in that morbidly unhealthy frame of mind when it seems unbearable to have to speak to others. The only person I cared to see was dear old Martha, for she would cry with me, though she, too, scolded me for not trying to bear up better.

But Lucia came : the moment she heard the dreadful tidings she left all her joys behind her, and packed up a trunk, and came as quick as steam and horseflesh would bring her. Nothing could exceed her gentle, sweet, sympathising manner. She took my heart by storm. It is true she was the means of making my tears gush forth again, but they were not the same bitter tears of desolation and despair, for I felt I had in her a true supporting heart to lean on. Poor old Martha had indeed given ma hers; but she was old, Lucia was new, and Lucia was more of my age, being nineteen whilst I was sixteen. So to Lucia I clung. Shall I tell you what she was like? Lucia was just a little above the middle height for girls. She had a most lovely figure, vith beautiful arms, hands, and feet The lines of her bosom were singularly beautiful, she was full there without being too plump, and her breasts seemed things of life She had a waist naturally small but not in the least waspish, and from this her hips gradually and gracefully expanded to a most exquisite fulness Her head was small, and beautifully poised on a throne of snow. But her face was too exquisite. Not only had she the most lovely dark brown eyes. most perfect nose, mouth and teeth, but her expression was for ever changing. It was my delight to feast upon her personal beauty, and I knew not which to admire most in her, for each point seemed perfection, and there seemed nothing to praise at the expense of something else Lucia might be compared with another girl as a whole, with me for instance, (and I have often been taken for her sister; but you could not say of her, she has lovely arms, feet, hands, breasts, etc

I shall not refer to our dear Mr Penwick and his legal lore, for I am not writing these memoirs from what may be called a public point of view, but rather as a history of my most private thoughts, ideas and deeds, and truly I fear that Mrs. Grundy would never permit her dear sons and daughters to peruse so much naughty description as I shall have to give, however much she might like to have the private reading of it herself!

But of Lucia, and of the lessons she gave me, and of the practice I made of them, I shall write as fully as I can, nor shall I in any way allow my pen to be prudish. I am going to tell the truth, the whole truth, and nothing but the truth, as they say in the courts of law, and as truth, to be truth, must be naked, so shall I be to my readers: and may there be many to admire my charms and appreciate them!

CHAPTER II

THE SOWING OF THE SEED

It was impossible for our house to remain long plunged in the depths of desolation, when once so sweet, amiable, and lovely a girl, as Lucia, had come into it. Naturally of a most loving and sympathetic disposition, she had, at first, been greatly grieved at the sad loss she had herself sustained by the deaths of a loving aunt and uncle. The almost tragic nature of their deaths had also a naturally inspiring effect upon her, and she was as subdued and tearful almost as Martha and I, but in less than a day she saw that if she were to be of any use she must overcome her own feelings, so as the better to raise our spirits. At first all our conversation was of the beloved parents, now, as I fondly thought, gone to eternal bliss in Heaven. Without stating her belief on this subject, Lucia rather encouraged mine; in fact she showed the greatest tact in gently leading my thoughts from the dark grave, and the darker secrets beyond it, to this world, and its multiplicity of pleasures and delights. She insisted on our taking good long walks. The weather was open and pleasant All nature seemed to be in accord with us—everything was well grown, but had still to reach full development. We ourselves, Lucia and I, were as it were in this condition too. It was impossible not to feel the effects of the lovely beauty of the country, of the sweet fresh air, of the song of the birds, and with exercise came back a more elastic state of health, and as my body improved in health so did my mind. Lucia in old times had sneered at beetles, and weeds, and stones, and rubbish, as she called the results of my natural history rambles, but now she appeared to take a delight in all I had to tell her about these things. I do not believe she knew a word of science, but she was so quick and intelligent, and seemed so anxious to learn, that I soon found myself growing quite excited in my eagerness to teach her, and if I referred to my dead parents it would be merely to tell Lucia what they had said about these matters, not to rail and lament as I had first done. So some three weeks passed away, and July was upon us, with hotter sun and warmer air. We used to be glad to find some glade in the woods, near a purling brook. where we could sit or lie down on the grass, and talk. One day when thus situated Lucia said :

" Susan ! do you intend to live here all your life ? "

" Well! " I answered, " I suppose so : where should I go ? and why should I not stay here ? "

" Oh ! " she said, " **now**, my dear,

without meaning to be at all rude to you, I don't think I could live here much longer."

"Oh! Lucia! You are not thinking, I hope, of going away yet! What should I do without you, my own darling cousin!" and I began to cry.

"There! There!" said she, putting her arm round my waist and kissing me, "I would not have said that if I had had any idea it would have made you cry, darling What I meant was, this is such a lonely spot! you never see a soul here from morning to night I declare I have been here nearly a month, and except old Penwich, I have not seen a single gentleman inside the house. Are there no families, with young men, living near enough to have discovered the lovely violet, called Susan Aked, who hides her beauteous charms in these secluded groves?"

She spoke half in earnest, half in jest, so said :—

"Now Lucia! don't make fun of me. I may live in a very secluded spot, but I don't see why you should find fault with people for not taking notice of such an insignificant girl as myself.

"But Susan! you are not insignificant. You are perfectly lovely, if you only knew it! now! let me speak! If you saw more people you could not help noticing, if no-one happened to tell you, that you are beautiful. Yes, beautiful! your eyes are something perfect, and so is your face. You have lips which no man can resist longing to kiss! you have a lovely figure, a perfect bust, or one which will soon be perfect when your breasts have grown a little more full; as it is I can see plainly through your dress that the high, hideous, stiff stays you wear cover two most charming little globes. Ah! why don't you get others, like mine for instance, which give all necessary support without preventing the rounded globes being seen? It is really a shame to spoil a bosom like yours, and a girl ought to take care of charms which have so powerful an influence over the imaginations of men.

"Oh goodness! Lucia! how you do run

on! Now do you think I care a straw what men may think of me! As for my stays, poor mamma bought them for me, and I think she was good enough judge of what I required."

"Ah! bless you, Susan dear! now I would not mind betting that, had poor aunt Maria lived to see you in society, she would soon have looked to your being dressed so as to show off all your lovely points to advantage."

"But suppose I don't care for society, and never wish to go into it."

"Oh! but Susan! you are talking of what you know nothing about. In a girl like you society means great admiration, and who is there who does not like to be admired?"

"Well! I don't care about it for one!"

"My dear child, for you are a child and nothing else in spite of all your science, and botany, and stuff, you have been so buried here, that unknown to yourself, you have grown up in complete ignorance that there is a world of men and women about you, and that some day, perhaps not far off now, you will have to take your place in that world. When you do, you will, I venture to prophesy, very soon find out what a charm there is in being admired. But, as I asked you before, are there no young men in these parts?"

"No! Lucia! I don't believe there are. We lived so very quietly, that I suppose if there are any such creatures, they never found us out. Our parish is quite a small one, and, as you may have seen in church, there are very few people in it, and no gentry. Papa used to be called 'The Squire.'"

"And you actually contemplate without horror the idea of living here by yourself all your life?"

"Oh, no! I hope you will come sometimes and see me, Lucia I shall ask Gladys, too Besides, I have old Martha, and I have my birds, and beasts, and flowers in the summer; my piano and my books in the winter; and my poor people to look after You have no idea of how very busy I am usually."

"But Martha won't be always with you. Gladys and I, I am sure, would be glad to come and stay with you sometimes; but, Susan dearest, I know Gladys well, and she would soon mope to death here where she would see noone of the opposite sex. Besides, her tastes are not half so countryfied as mine, and I declare to you that, much as I love you, I do not think I could live here much longer without being tired of myself, and even of you. Women require men just as much as men require women. If you had some handsome, agreeable young squires down here it would be pleasant enough to spend the days flirting in the fields and woods with them, but there is not a soul!"

"My goodness! Lucia! how you do care about men! Now I declare I should not mind it, I never saw another in my life!"

"That is because you have never known a town, my dear Susan. You have never known what is to be wooed! You don't know the pleasure of courtship. You don't know what it is to have a man worshipping the very ground you have walked on In fact you have never even dreamt of love "

I was silent.

" Well! " she continued, " now have you? "

" I really do not understand a word of what you are talking, about, Lucia. To me a man is nothing, and as for love, except the love of my parents, or of you, or of dear old Martha, I know nothing. You mean something, I am sure, of which I have never heard. Of course a husband loves his wife, a parent his child, but I can't see what there is in such love for anybody to rave above as you do! "

" Have you never read any novels, nor any love stories, Susan? " she went on.

" No! my father and mother said they were foolish stuff."

" I have heard them say so. And have you not even Sir Walter Scott or Shakespeare in the house?

" Shakespeare we have, I know; but it is locked up in papa's study, in the glass bookcase. I have never read it."

"Ah! then read ' Romeo and Juliet,' and you may perhaps learn a secret or two "

" The secret of love? But what is this curious secret, Lucia?"

" Well now, Susan? answer me! you are a girl, are you not? "

" Yes, of course I am."

" Of course you are! But why ' of course? "

" Well! because I am, I suppose! I was born so. I dont't know any other reason."

" Well! but there is a very good reason, if you only knew it. Why should you be formed different to a man, for instance? Can you tell me that, sweet Susan? "

" I don't know, but what difference is there? Lucia stared at me with very open eyes

" Oh! come! Susan! you don't mean to pretend that you have lived so long without knowing that there are most marked differences between a man and a woman?" so saying she reached out her hand, and lightly placed it in my lap, pressing her fingers on the part between my thighs. " Now are you not immensely different from a man *here?*"

Of course I knew I was. I knew that a man was not formed there as I was, but I tell the truth if I say I did not then know *exactly* what the formation of a man was

" And have you never wondered why you should be formed here as you are?" keeping her hand still pressing between my thighs, whilst she gently stroked the place with her long taper fingers.

" No indeed I have not! but, Lucia darling, don't do that!"

" Why not! you are a girl and I am another. Surely one girl may touch another there? what harm is there in it?"

" I don't know whether there is any harm, but oh!."

" What's the matter? said Lucia, her colour rising slightly

" My dear girl! oh! for goodness sake take away your hand! you are tickling me dreadfully! oh! now! don't go on, or you will make me scream!"

" Scream away my pet!" said Lucia,

laughing, " you may spend your breath, if you like, that way, but I mean to make you spend something else before I have done!"

I did not understand her; in fact the pleasure she gave me was so intense, and at the same time seemed to me so shameful, that between the two feelings I was nearly distracted. In vain did I try to tear myself away from her. Lucia held me tight with one arm, whilst she half lay upon me, laughing and looking into my eyes as if she expected to see something she wanted to find in them. Very soon the tickling reached such a point, that I felt that if I did not find some way of relieving myself I must faint. Lucia observed my rapidly weakening struggles, for she said :

" Ah! my dear! if your dress were not so thick, and if you had not on two petticoats, I would have made you come before this; but I don't think it is far off all the same!"

As she spoke I felt myself as it were jump under her hand, a thrill, a throb shot through all that region, a delicious sense of some pent up flood bursting the ever lightening bonds which had held it back, made itself distinctly felt, and so great a sensation of delightful languor took hold of me that I could not resist giving vent to a grateful, " How nice that is ! "

Lucia took her hand off, and throwing herself completely on me, she pressed me enthusiastically in her arms, kissing me with the most passionate affection.

" Ah ! " she said, " so my darling Susan is sensitive to pleasure ! I thought a girl made like her must be. Oh ! Susan ! Susan ! would that I were a man ! would I not make you happy ! and myself too ! "

" Well," said I, " please do get off me, Lucia ! I am nearly choking, and your weight is perhaps heavier than you think. Ah ! now I can breathe ! oh ! goodness ! I am all wet ! " Lucia burst into a fit of laughter.

" Wet ! are you ? of course you are, darling ! I have made you spend ! but Lord ! if I had been a man, and had been slithering into you, instead of first tickling your cunnie with my hand, I would have made you spend a dozen times! "

" I don't know what you mean," said I, " and I don't know what you mean by spending."

" Why! bless you girl! do you mean to tell me that you have never tickled yourself, there? " laying her hand once more on my lap, but taking it away again immediately, " in bed, until what you call the wet, and I call spend came? "

" Never! " said I.

" Ah! that is just because your thoughts have never rightly turned to love, my pet! I really do believe you are as ignorant and as innocent as I thought you were only pretending to be! I see I have a great deal to teach you! and I will teach you, too! But see, it is getting time for us to be going home, and I dare say you would like to put on some dry drawers "

But although I pretended to be of the same mind, yet no sooner had Lucia begun to rise than I pushed her over, and made a grab at her, caught her, turned her on her back, and putting my hand between her thighs, I began to treat her as she had treated me. Instead of struggling, she lay perfectly quiet, looking up into my glowing face, saying !—" Well! what are you up to now, Susan ? "

" I am going to punish you and treat you the same way you treated me! and see if you like being tickled nearly to death ! "

" Oh! " said she, " I defy you to tickle me. You don't know how to do it."

" Perhaps not so well as you do, darling! but I will try, any way! "

Lucia had not nearly so thick a material in her dress as I had, and she had on the lightest of petticoats and shift. I could distinctly feel the soft yielding charm under my moving fingers and even thought I could trace the deep line which marked her sex.

She lay quite quiet for about half a minute, when she suddenly gave a little start. " Ah! ha! Miss! I don't tickle you, I suppose! "

" No! not a bit! "

I continued my movements. Lucia's colour began to rise, her bosom to heave; I could feel the elasticity of her breasts as they rose and sank under mine I began to feel a fresh tickling myself, though her hand was no longer in my lap, and the caressing of the charming and beautiful girl began to fascinate me. Still, except that one little start, she showed no outward signs of being tickled by me. But all of a sudden she clasped me round the waist and exclaimed —

" You have got on to it at last! keep your fingers moving just there Oh. my darling! my darling! ah, that's it! Oh, Susan! Ah! Ah! Oh my God! oh how heavenly! A little quicker, darling! Ah now, quick, quick! harder harder, ah-h-h! ah-h-h! There! "

The increasing excitement excited me still more. Whether it was sympathetic or not I don't know, but as she exclaimed "there!" I felt myself gone again, and a fresh flood once more soiled the purity of my drawers. I sunk on to Lucia's bosom for a moment, and we both lay quite still. At last I raised my head and looked at her. Her face was flushed, but she had her eyes closed. and her lips slightly parted, and looked so still that I thought she had fainted Alarmed I shook her gently. "Lucia, Lucia!" I cried

"What is it. darling?" she said languidly, " oh, you dearest pet! what pleasure, what exquisite pleasure you gave me!"

Reassured by hearing her speak I recovered my equanimity, and jokingly asked her : " Well, now! did I not tickle you?"

" That you did, darling! and right well too."

"But you defied me to be able to do so!"

Lucia laughed. She caught me again in her arms, and said :—" Ah, Susanna mia! there is such a thing as having a little fox to catch a lovely goose! But come, oh dear! I must have spent a cup full! I am drenched!'

"And so am I," said I, " for I spent, as you call it, again, when I was just finishing you off!"

Lucia, who was on her feet, once more caught me in her arms and said :—

"Ah, Susan! to leave you here where you can never know a man would be to sin! You must come and live with me, and learn how to use and enjoy the exquisite and sensitive charms you are endowed with. You are just the girl to form into a real priestess of Venus!

CHAPTER III

GERMINATION

We walked home quickly, my little terrier Spot moving close behind us, and sniffing at each of us, as though he smelt something very nice. Lucia laughed when she noticed it, and said he was a very sensible little dog When we got home she took him into her room with her, and I believe Spot had a very good time of it for him. At least, I know that on another occasion when he was in my room, he came whilst I was changing my drawers and licked my cunnie in the most pleasant manner, a thing he had never offered to do before. Lucia knew a thing or two.

When I went downstairs I found Mrs. Warmart talking in a most animated manner to Lucia, so animated, indeed, that I could not but think she had been having a good glass or two

" Ah, here the darling comes," she said, as I entered the room, " we were just saying, Miss Susan, that you are old enough, and big enough, to be showing your beauties to the world For what's the good of a girl made like you hiding herself in the woods You are getting old enough to be thinking of a handsome young lover "
" I dare say," said the talkative old lady, winking at Lucia, " Miss Susan often wakes in the morning, and wonders where the brave young fellow is, who she dreamt was abed with her "

" Not she! " said Lucia, " you never knew such a girl, Martha! I dont't believe she ever thinks of a lover at all! She certainly does not dream of one. Beetles and butterflies, and old bits of stone are more her way "

"Ah well!" replied Martha, "Miss Susan may have a butterfly yet for a lover, and I'll be bound she will find he has a good pair of slones with him."

Lucia burst with laughter.

"Aye! and she will like feeling and examining them too! won't she, Martha?"

"In course she will, the darling! But look at the pretty innocent! She don't know from Adam what we are talking about!"

"Well, I don't!" said I, " and what is more I don't want to. I detest the idea of lovers, and should never have thought of such a creature, but for Lucia's chat."

"Ah well, dearie!" said Martha, "believe me, woman's comfort and blessing lies in man, and just as a man ain't perfect without his woman, so is a woman wanting until she has her man, to fit like into her."

Lucia clapped her hands.

' That is it exactly," she cried, "just like one of your beloved flowers, Susan! when the male part fits exactly and sweetly, and nicely, and lovingly into the female."

"I don't understand you," said I bewildered, " how can a man fit into me?"

" Oh! " said Martha, " Miss Lucia can tell you, Miss Susan dear, and most girls of your age would know it too, without going to bed with a man."

" The idea! " cried I

" Well! when you are married won't you have your husband in bed with you? " said Martha laughing.

" I'll never be married! "

" Fiddle-sticks! " cried Martha, " it would be a sin for you not to be married, you'll never know pleasure without, and I can tell'ye, young ladies," said she, sinking her voice to a whisper, " that until a girl marries a man she don't know what pleasure means. I've known girls, young ladies, quite afeared the day of the first night they were going to sleep with their husbands, frightened to go to bed, thinking something dreadful was going to happen, and next morning die of laughing at their odd fears, and longing for night to come, so as they might have some more fun."

Old Penwick's bell rang and put a stop to Martha's chat, and I turned to Lucia, and said :

" Really, Lucia, you must tell me all about men and wives, and teach me, because I feel like a fool when you and Martha go on so. I don't understand one atom! though perhaps," I continued, as a bright thought struck me, "men tickle their wives as you tickled me this afternoon, and that is what Martha meant? "

" I tell you what, Susan darling," she replied, " I won't tell you now, but I'll come to you after you have gone to bed, for I don't want to chat on matters it would be difficult to drop, if that old lady came in suddenly atop of us. I think she has had a little too much to drink, and is merry; another time she might speak quite another kind of talk. But come upstairs. I want you to try on my stays, for positively you must leave off wearing such barbarous ones as yours, and we must go to Worcester to-morrow, and see what the shops there can produce, and if we can't get what I fancy there, I must write to London for some to be sent down for you to fit on. Such lovely bubbies as these," said she laying her two hands on my breasts, " must not be squashed flat and be displaced, but be left free to rise and fall."

So upstairs we trotted to my room. The first thing Lucia saw on entering was my wet drawers spread out on the bed.

" Good gracious, Susan! why did you leave those things there?"

" Why? what harm if I did?"

" Because if old Mother Warmart should have happened to see them, her suspicions would at once have been roused, and goodness only knows what she would have thought—very likely that you had been had by a man."

" Well, Lucia dear, I am sorry; but indeed I never thought there was any reason to hide anything I did. I know you meant no harm, and I am sure I did not, when we had the tickling match."

" My dear, let me tell you that, although all the world does what we did, and a good deal more too, yet, just as our cunnies are covered up from sight, so are the deeds done by them. So we will put your drawers away. They are nearly dry, and if they stain at all, it will be very slightly. Martha will not guess the truth."

As she spoke she took up the garment, and held it out in front of her to examine its state of humidity.

" Oh Lord, what drawers! Why! they are only cut up behind. You ought to have them cut up to the waistband in front too, Susan."

" Why? "

" Because how on earth could your lover feel you if you had things like this on? Instead of finding a nice charming bush, and a hot little twot ready and eager for his hand and probing finger, this wretched calico would be in his way! And how on earth could you manage an *al fresco* poke if you wore these drawers? "

" Well, considering I would die sooner than let a man touch me there, I don't see it makes any difference. I am afraid I am extremely ignorant; but I don't know what an *al fresco* poke means, Lucia!"

" Ah, well! you'll learn, and soon too! I'll take care of that. But now off with your dress and petticoats I want to see how my stays will fit you."

So saying, she commenced, with her usual agility, to undo her dress, and before I had got mine half unhooked, she was standing before me in her chemise and drawers only.

" There! " she cried, standing in front of me, " look, Susan. Do you see how free my breasts are? Nothing to compress them. Each in its own little nest. They don't require support, for they are as firm as rocks, and hard as marble. Feel them! "

I did. Strange to say I had never seen a girl's bosom naked before. I had no girl-companions, and the only youthful bosom I had ever seen bare, was my own. I was immensely moved at the sight of the glowing bosom before me, so white and so beautiful! I put my hand, first on one and then on the other, of the exquisite globes, and felt a great pleasure thrill through me, as I plessed them. Though not literally "hard as marble," they were decidedly extremely firm and elastic, and their shapes were perfect. Lucia was right to consider her bubbies lovely, for they were.

"Kiss them, darling," said she.

I did so with pleasure. It seemed to me as though some new revelation were opening up to me, for I never should have imagined there could have been anything so delightful in a girl's bosom, had I been asked about it, before Lucia exposed hers to me.

"Now, come! quick! off with that dress, you dreadful old slow coach!" she cried to me. "Here, let me help you."

In a moment she had me in the same state as herself. I saw at once the hideousness of my stays, which were much too high, and much too rigid, and which fitted neither breast, waist, nor hips. Lucia quickly had them unlaced, and opening the top of my chemise, which she complained of as being too high in the neck, she slipped it off me, so that it fell to the ground, and except for my drawers I was naked before her.

" Oh, the little beauties! " she exclaimed, "oh, the charming, charming little bubbies! How nice, how firm? Why Susan, I declare I should never have thought you had such perfections. Those beastly, disgraceful stays must be burnt, you must never put them on again. Bubbies like these," she continued, pressing them in her hand alternately, causing me to feel my cunnie tickling, all on fire again, " are not meant to be shut up in a box, but put under a glass case, so that they may be seen, and their full beauty appreciated. What lovely, lovely, little rosebuds. Like tiny coral marbles, topping little mountains of snow I must kiss and nibble them."

And down went her lips first on to one, and then on to the other, whilst her naughty hand again sought the cunnie she had taught to tickle at her touch. Impatiently she tried to find the division of my drawers, and at last did so, but so far back that she could not get at what she sought after.

"What beastly drawers!" she cried, "but I won't be baffled!"

She ran to the dressing table, took a pair of scissors, and, before I knew what she was at, she had the point through the calico, and ripped it down

Throwing the scissors down, she clasped me round the waist with her left arm, and again attacked my bosom with her lips, whilst her hand, having no obstacle to oppose it, took possession of my fleshy motte and throbbing cunnie; She was altogether too delicious for me to wish to oppose her With the palm of her hand she pressed the rising, elastic cushion above the deep line, whilst her middle finger slipped in up to its knuckle, and was completely buried in my rapidly moistening cunnie

"How nice! what a sweet, sweet little cunt! How velvety and soft inside; how quickly it responds to my touch. Oh! what would not Charlie give to get his prick into such a lovely shrine of love, etc., etc." She rambled on, moving her finger up and down, occasionally withdrawing it to seek another more ticklesome spot, between my cunnie's lips, near the top, and then pushing it in deep, in and out, until I felt ready to die with the pleasure she caused me. At last she felt a convulsive little throb, which told her that I was very nearly *come*. She clasped me to her bosom, her breast against mine, swerving her body a little from side to side, so that her bubbies swept on mine, backwards and forwards, her nipples catching on mine, and tickling them immensely, whilst, with her lips open and sucking my mouth, I felt her moist tongue darting in and out between my teeth.

All this takes longer to write than it did to act. I felt myself growing faint with exquisite languor. I could see nothing. One vast pleasure seemed to embrace me on every side. I was all on fire, and suddenly, with almost a pang of voluptuousness, I spent all over Lucia's hand and wrist. Keeping her finger still gently moving, and gently pressing my motte, she drew back her head, looked at me, and said ; " Now, Susan! was not that a nice one?"

" Indeed it was," I said, feeling almost unable to peak from excess of emotion.

" Well, a man would give you fifty times as much pleasure with his hand, and a thousand times more with his prick! "

Then she suddenly left me, ran for my towel, wiped her hand, and then commenced to gently wipe me between my thighs.

" Ah! what a pearl of a cunnie," she cried. " what a lovely brush what a lot of silky hair you have here, darling! what a splendid motte! a regular cushion for love to repose upon! so elastic, yet so soft! Gods! why am I not a man now that I might enjoy all these beauties."

" I almost wish you were, Lucia darling! " I said, laughing, " for I am getting most particularly curious to know what new bliss there can be in store for me But really! Do you know I believe you are making me lose every particle of modesty I ever possessed."

And I laughed again.

"Ah! Susanna mia! Modesty is the shift which covers the cunts of us girls; a useful garment enough when we go abroad into society, and one which no wise woman would care to be without, but in intimate friendship, like ours, it becomes useless, nay, like those wretched drawers of yours, and those abominable stays, all absolute bars to freedom and ease. I would not offend against modesty in public, but with you, or my lovers, I think it is a thing to be put off, and I like to be natural woman on such occasions, naked as the ungloved hand. Ah! happy thought! Let us strip altogether now, and have a good look at the shapes beneficent nature has given us!"

She threw away the towel, slid first one shoulder, gleaming like polished marble, then the other out of her shift, unbuttoned her drawers, and let them fall to the ground, whisked off her garters, pulled off her stockings, and, in less time than you could count ten, dear, and I hope fair reader, there was Lucia as naked as she was born. and as beautiful in her nudity as Venus fresh risen from the sea.

I, as usual, was slow In every step I was hesitating. A struggle between consciousness and innocency seemed to occur every time I was asked to take a pace more forward on the road to the fulfilment of the sacrifices to love, though I am bound to say that the struggle became weaker and more weak as every forward bound brought with it new and more exquisite enjoyment.

But Lucia could not tolerate slowness; she came and added her nimble assistance, and in a moment I was, like her, in a state of perfect nature. A kind of bastard shame, however, took possession of me. Not even before Martha had I been accustomed to be so completely naked as I now was, and instinctively I put one hand over my motte, whilst with the other hand and arm I attempted to hide my bosom, I felt myself blushing, too, under the keen gaze of Lucia's beaming eyes.

" Oh! the charming, charming **Venus de Medici!** " she cried, clapping her hands. " Don't stir from that position, Susan dear; **you** are lovely, lovely. I want to walk round, and observe and admire you from all points of view. Don't stir. Just lift your hand a little bit off your motte! That's it. Ah! I can see in you what that Venus was not permitted by her sculptor to show, a sweetest little cunnie retreating between voluptuous thighs, and shaded by the most silky-haired nest I have ever seen," etc., etc.

And so she chattered on, walking round and round me, putting me into various attitudes, and exclaiming, in what sounded language of exaggeration, at all the perfect beauties she saw in me. According to her I had the very finest shape she had ever seen; the most glossy, white, smooth skin, without spot, a girl could possibly have; a bosom for a god to revel in; thighs to clasp a Lazarus with, and bring him straight back to life; whilst my cunnie was an object so perfect to outward appearance that Venus herself would have envied me. All this time I was taking equal stock of her, and of her beauties. Ah reader! would I had the pen of a poet, that I could do Lucia justice. I only half listened to her ravings about myself, so absorbed was I in gazing on her Every movement a verse of poetry, and every charm a blaze of beauty.

My room was lighted by one high window, and on one side of this window was the press in which I hung my clothes. It had a broad door, and that door was a large mirror, fully six feet high. I was a girl of nature. Had I ever bathed near this mirror I should have often seen myself naked reflected in it, but as a matter of fact, it never struck me that it was worth while to take the trouble to walk from the corner of my room, where my bath was always placed for me, to look at my naked charms in this glass. I used it occasionally when I dressed with extra care to go to church, or to go into Worcester, or to Malvern, but I was not much given to admire myself in any glass.

I had no idea that I was beautiful, and I did not care for my face. But Lucia, who was very artistic in her taste, and no mean hand with brush and pencil, at once saw an opportunity for a pretty picture. She drew the curtains of the window so as to form only a broad ckink, through which light enough would shine to illumine any object near the window, but not so much as to cause any powerful reflections from the walls, and then so placed herself and me, side by side opposite the mirror I was delighted. I had never seen anything so perfectly lovely as we looked in that glass. Two naked nymphs with the most graceful forms, glowing with life, showing all that makes beauty most bewitching, rosy cheeks, cherry lips, glistening eyes, necks and arms and thighs of polished marble, breasts looking each a little askance, tipped with rosy nipples, skins as pure as snow but lighted with the faintest rosy tints, as of light reflected from a dying sunset sky, and forms which shone out against the dark background, sharp, yet soft lined, and clear as the light of day. Oh! what a mistake artists make in failing to ornament the soft rising triangle beneath the curve of their beauties' bellies, with the dark curling hair that Nature has provided, surely to enhance the lovely slope which leads to the entrance of the Temple of Love. The contrast afforded by this dark, bushy, little hill, and the surrounding white plain of the belly, or the snowiness of the round voluptuous thighs is really exquisite. And why do painters and sculptors neglect the soft, inturning folds, which form that deep, quiet looking line, that retreats into the depths between the thighs, half hidden by the curling locks, but plain in nature, and to deprive woman of which would take from her her very essense? They don't do it to men. I have seen statues and pictures in which all that a man has, prick, balls, bush, are represented with striking fidelity, if partly idealised : why then should it be indecent to picture woman's most powerful charm. It cannot surely be said that what men most prize in her, is too ugly to be drawn or moulded. Lucia was wild over her lovely picture, as she called it. She put herself and me into various attitudes, and admired, as indeed did I, all that the faithful glass reflected I could not help noticing, however, that her form showed great matureness than mine, but she told me that there were few girls of my age who could compare with me in that quality, and that in a very short time, some few months, my shoulders and hips and limbs would be as round as hers.

" As for your bosom, Susan, I would not wish to see it one atom more developed. I should like you to keep these exquisite little bubbies just as they are. Let them grow just a trifle firmer perhaps, but not one atom larger See! a man's hand could hardly completely cover one They have just sufficient prominence to fulfil the law of beauty, and they look so imploringly at one as though to say : ' Please squeeze me! Please kiss me ! ' Your motte I should like to see just a trifle more plump, another quarter of an inch rise would do it no harm, and be more agreeable for a man to feel when he drives home the last inch, or squeezes in the last line after the short digs."

"I am beginning to understand," said I; "but Lucia, now you have the opportunity, no one is near, tell me all about a man, and what it is he does to one. What are short digs?"

"I'll sleep with you to-night, my pet," she said, kissing me; "but I shall have so much to tell that I won't spoil the fun by beginning now. Besides, when once I get on that topic I shall get so wild, I know that nothing but my copious and repeated spending will relieve me, or you either," said she, archly laughing and stroking my cunnie most delightfully. "Now," she added, "come, dress and put on my stays, and I'll put on yours, and we will go and exhibit ourselves to Mrs. Warmart."

Lucia made me put on her stays and dress, and she herself put on mine. We were much of the same height and build. only, as I have before said, she was everywhere a little fuller, more rounded, so to say, than I. Both she and I were surprised to find that her dress was not in the least too full in the bosom for me, and it was not simply the stays which made the fit apparently correct, for my own bubbies quite filled up the bags in them; in fact, had they been made for me, her stays could not have fitted better. But it was different with her when she put on mine. Her poor darling. lovely bubbies were simply squashed out flat, and yet she could hardly get my dress to fasten over her bosom.

" Oh! " she cried, " the brutal instrument of torture! I will wear it for a few minutes just to show Martha, but no longer. After that, Susan, my dear, we will change again. I wonder how you could have endured such a strait jacket as this, or how on earth your bubbies ever came to be so sweetly round and pointed as they really are. Mine are crushed! " Then looking me over, she exclaimed at the beauty of my figure, which was now shown off. she said, to perfection, and had a chance of appearing at last as it should. We ran downstairs to Martha, who, busy at some household work, looked up and mistook me for Lucia.

Lucia was delighted.

"Ah! Susan, I told you so. Now look, Mrs. Warmart, I am not going to let Susan wear those abominable stays any longer. I know I have a good figure, yet first look at me! Did you ever see such a lout of a girl as I look! Positively you would never think I had any breast at all, and I declare I hardly thought Susan had any either. Yet see! Just feel the lovely little ducks! Firm, round, elastic; such a pair of pretty doves with little rosy bills! It is downright shameful to crush them in such a wooden box of a corset as this. I know my breast is actually hurt under it."

"Well, you see, miss, it was all her ma's wish. She neve liked Miss Susan to look grown up and developed."

'But why? why on earth? Anyone could see that she must be quite ripe. Look at her hips."

" Ah, well! She had a good reason, my dear young lady "

" Perhaps she had, and herhaps she had as good a reason why poor Susan should be condemned to wear drawers which must be exceedingly incommodious at certain times, to say the least of it ! "

" Well, yes, miss. There was the same reason for that too I hardly like to say before Miss Susan, because she is innocent like. Yet she ought to know to be on her guard."

" Well, Martha, since Susan is quite old enough to know what is what, you might tell us the grand reason."

"Well, miss, when Master Charlie Althair lived at The Broads, people said that there were not two greater pests than him and Jack Cocklade, who lived in Leigh. I do believe Master Charlie got credit for doing more than he did, but all the people complained that no sooner did their daughters get fledged than either he or Jack would be into them, and that ripe maidenheads could not be found, high or low! What Master Charlie did not pluck, Jack did. No one ever brought an affiliation case against Master Charlie, but Jack is known to be father of ever so many love children. Poor Miss Mary Essex was raped by one or other of em in her own father's field, not half a mile from home. I believe that it was Jack who did it, but there was a great noise a little time after, when she and Master Charlie were caught by Mr. Essex hard at it in one of his barns. They were caught in the very act, and it was that which caused Mrs. Althair, who had no idea until then what a ively lad he was, to go away from The Broads. I believe she had to pay up handsomely for that little spree of her son's, and being a very strict and straight lady, she could not face the people after her disgrace, as she called it. Jack, indeed, got imprisoned for his share, because Miss Mary Essex confessed he had had her before Master Charlie and against her will; but he was let off pretty easy because she had to admit that she did love, being had by Master Charlie. This happened some five or six years ago, and poor Mrs. Aked got such a shock she wouldn't let Miss Susan out by herself, nor allow her to have her drawers divided at all. But poor Miss Suzan complained she could not do her jobs easy when she had to unbutton her drawers behind, so she had them cut as you find them now."

I saw that Lucia was dying with internal laughter, and I felt beetroot-red with shame. But more and more I understood what was said about Charlie Althair and Jack Cocklade, and why my drawers were so made as to cover my cunnie completely when not partly loosened.

" Well, Martha," said Lucia, " I think Susan can defend herself in future. So anyhow I am going to take it on myself to drive her to Worcester to-morrow to look for a decent pair of stays, and as she is so uncomfortable in her drawers, we will cut them up in front and make them as they should be."

" I'm much afraid you can't go to Worcester to-morrow, my dear young lady, because the horse has gone to be shod, and won't be back till to-morrow afternoon. Bill Coachman is going to Hereford to see his wife's mother, and said he would not be here till to-morrow evening, but the brougham will be ready for you the next day after "

"Well, so be it We can wait a day. Come, Susan. Now for goodness' sake let me have my stays again! "

So off we trotted upstairs once more. I admired myself in the glass, until Lucia had taken off her dress, and then, with a sigh, I yielded her own, and once more clad myself in my old habiliments.

Agreeably to her promise Lucia came to my bedroom after Martha and the servants had gone to bed. She sprang into my bed and clasped me in her arms and kissed me repeatedly, and said :—

" Oh, Susan! we will have such a night of it. I'll tell you all you want to know, and I will show you more, and I will prove to you that it is downright folly to lose years of youth, which can be so well turned to profit by using the charms and senses nature has given you. But let me put my hand between your legs, darling. Ah! that is it. Now I'll just slip my finger in this delicious little cunt. You do the same to me! "

" Ah! now am I not nice, and hot, and soft inside? "

" Indeed you are, Lucia, like velvet warmed before the fire."

" And so are you, darling; but now we won't have any tickling yet. Now I will tell you about men."

" Ah do! I am dying with curiosity, Lucia."

" Well now, just here," said she, pressing her thumb on a spot above my cunnie, " a man's thing grows out from him. That thing is called his prick, or his yard, or his tool, or his Johnnie, or half a hundred other names. When it is not standing, it is about two and a half or three inches long, all small, and soft, and flabby, and wrinkled, but when it stands it is seven or eight inches long, as big round as my wrist, and hard as iron. A most formidable weapon to thrust into the poor little belly of a girl!"

"But what makes it stand, Lucia?" I asked, breathless with unaccountable emotion, and feeling a strange shiver pass through me at the notion of such a monstrous thing being thrust into my belly

"Oh! there are physical reasons for that which I won't go into now, but the actual cause of its standing is desire. When a man thinks of a girl and wants to have her, up goes his prick, it lifts itself with pride and power, and becomes just like a bar of iron covered from end to end with a thick, soft, velvety skin If you were to take a good hold of one in that condition you could move your hand up and down, without the skin slipping from under your fingers, just like you can move the skin of a cat on its body!"

"Really! How curious!"

"Yes Well, there it stands. But it is not exactly round It is slightly broader than it is deep, so to say, and it has the most curious-looking head imaginable. It is something like a cherry at the end, and in the tip is a little hole, out of which comes the dangerous stuff which makes the little babies!"

"Oh, my!"

"Well; the head is shaped there like a bell. It is blueish purple round the lower rim, which rim forms a regular shoulder. You can slip the moveable skin right off the head, and behind the shoulder, and there it will stay, unless it is forcibly put back again. Underneath the nose, as I will take it, of the prick, the moveable skin is fastened, not far behind the point, and when the stand or stiffness is gone out of the prick this fastening pulls the cap over its head again!"

"How very curious! how convenient!"

"Well, now; under the prick, nearly as far back, but not quite, as the place where it springs from, is a very curious, very wrinkled bag, in which the balls are—balls something like small eggs, and far nicer both to feel and see. I dearly love feeling a man's balls, and does not he like it, too? They feel slippery and hard, but you must take care not to squeeze them tight, as it hurts a man very much; but gently handling them, lifting them up with the tips of the fingers, and gently rolling them about in their bag, is most pleasing to every man, and if his prick has gone down, such treatment will quickly bring it back grand, and stiff, and big, and ready for work again."

"And what are his balls for, Lucia?" said I.

"Oh! his balls hold the stuff he spends when he fucks us, darling. A white, creamy looking stuff, like milk, only thicker, which spouts out in jets. I have seen Charlie Althair spout it three feet high."

"Charlie Althair!" exclaimed.

"Yes, darling. Charlie was my first love, and it was he who took my maidenhead. He is a grand fellow everywhere, and no girl could have him in her bed without going half mad over him. He is able to give extraordinary pleasure, and I ought to know, for I have had plenty of experience."

" Then there is a difference between men, that way, Lucia ? "

" Oh! there is indeed! Sometimes one gets hold of a fellow, well made in every respect, but an indifferent bed-fellow, not simply because he does not, or cannot give one enough, but because he does not know how to do it properly."

" And how should it be done properly, Lucia ? "

" I'll tell you, darling. Oh! if I only were a man! if only instead of this cunt I had a rattling, fine, big, long prick, as stiff as a poker, and a wellfurnished pair of balls hanging to it, I would show you, my Susan! I would show you what a real, good, unmistakeable fuck is ! I am just the one who knows how it should be done, to be well done."

" Ah, Lucia; but as you have no prick, and no balls, can't you tell me, all the same? I am dying to know."

" Ah, my sweet Susan is growing randy!

I know she is. I think a little bit of a spend would do her good! I tell you what," she said, her voice growing thick and hurried, as though emotion were choking her, " I will show you how a man gets on to you, and how he moves, and I will make you spend a dozen times! for, darling, I must either spend myself or burst! "

So saying, she pulled my chemise above my bubbies, and rolled it on my neck, and pulling up her own, and holding its end under her chin and on her bosom, she got between my knees.

" Open your thighs wide, darling, my darling! " she cried in a most excited manner. " Open your thighs! Draw up your knees! That is it. Oh my! a kingdom to have a prick now!" She sank on to my belly. She put one hand under my hips to raise them. The other she put round my neck. Her bubbies coincided with mine, I could feel their hard little nipples pressing into my breasts, whilst mine, equally hard, met her harder and more elastic globes. She pressed her bushy motte to mine, lifted me a little with her hand, and brought the two hot lips of her burning cunnie on to mine. Then she, as it were, sank her hips. The top of her cunt touched the bottom of mine, and then with a pressing upward sweep, she brought her cunnie all over mine from end to end of the slit. Down she swept again! Then up! Then down, until I thrilled through and through with extraordinary and untold pleasure. I felt her grasp growing tighter and tighter, her breathing became more and more hurried, her breasts crushed mine, they seemed to swell and become harder. Then, when she had come to the end of one of her long upward sweeps, she suddenly spent all over my motte. I could feel the hair there inundated. At the same moment she received my offering full on her cunnie as she swept down mine. This excited her immensely. and she redoubled her efforts to make the spasms come again. I clasped her to me. I returned the rain of furnace-like kisses she showered all over my face. I felt wild. Again and again we spent all over one another's cunts and bushes. I can't tell how many times, until at length drenched, breathless, and tired Lucia lay heavily on me, and for a moment we were motionless. Then, lifting her head, she kissed me in the most loving manner.

" My little darling! My own sweetest darling Susan! how did you like that? "

" Oh! Lucia, it was heavenly! Do it again, darling! " I cried clasping her between my thighs, and pressing my glowing cunt to hers

" Not just yet, dearest! no, Susan, I have come at least fifteen times, and you are wet as a drowned rat! indeed so am I! you naughty little girl! how you do spend! "

" You taught me," said I.

" Ah, yes! you are a darling and splendid pupil, my Susan, and a perfect mine of these pearls!" said she pointing to a drop depending from her bush, and which, when it dropped on to my thigh as she got off me, felt cold.

"Now," she continued, "come! get up! we must ablutionise."

We both got out of bed. Lucia dropped her chemise, and stood naked and beautiful before me. I did the same. She again exclaimed at what she called the extraordinary gracefulness of my figure, and again wished she was a man.

We washed one another's cunnies, and then, naked as we were, again got into bed, and with arms round one another's waists, and thighs locked in thighs, we pressed our bosoms together, and Lucia continued her instructions.

"Well, Susanna mia, that little bit of initiation was a nice little interlude, and imperfect as it was, it has shown you at least how you will have to lie when you are had, à la Adam and Eve, by a man, for you must not imagine for a moment that a man has only one way of fucking a girl. There are heaps of ways, all more or less nice, but to my simple mind the Adam and Eve is the best of all, because it is the most natural and the most perfect."

"But, Lucia darling," said I, "I have not a notion of what you mean by *Adam and Eve* as compared with other ways. You said you would tell me how a man should well do it with a girl, so as to be perfect in his action."

"Oh, my modest little mouse! Now, Susan, say fuck."

"I was not quite sure of the term. Lucia dearest. I did not mean to be over-particular. Well, tell me exactly how a man should fuck a girl, so as to give her the most complete pleasure. For my part, not knowing what it is like, I should imagine that the mere sensation of having so big a thing, as you say a man's prick is, inside one's cunt, would be rather disagreeable than otherwise. Why, even you, who have, you tell me, been fucked, have quite a thight little cunt. How on earth can such a small, narrow slit like this, take in a thing as thick as one's wrist? I can hardly believe it, or, if I do believe it, I can hardly fancy its being pleasant."

Lucia listened to me with a smiling face

She kissed me, and put her hand on my motte, slipping her finger up to her knuckles into my still throbbing cunnie.

"Yes, my Susan. Our cunts are, luckily for us and our lovers, small and tight. If they were not, neither they, nor we would have half the pleasure we do. I say we, because it won't be long now before you know what a delicious, deliriously rapturous and excessively delightful thing it is to be well and often fucked. Oh, dear, why have I not a prick? How easy it would be to show you, darling, far more easy than to explain!"

"Oh, Lucia! *do go on*! Tell me, Girl! you keep me actually on thorns of expectation!"

Lucia laughed, passed her finger deliciously two or three times up and down my cunnie, then took it out, and grasped my left breast in her hand, pressing it gently, as though she loved doing so.

"Well! Susan! here it goes. Now I'll do my best to describe what a man should do to give you the acme of pleasure. First of

all he should put his prick into your hand
It is a most thrilling thing to feel; oh! it is
delightful when you feel it from end to end.
Its hardness like iron; its soft velvety; skin,
its soft cushion-like head, and its shifting
hood; his grand balls in their wrinkled
silky, soft bag; and the thick rough bush
out of which this galaxy of manly charms
grows, all form objects of delight to the
hand that knows how to caress them, and
to the cunt which expects so soon to feel
their powerful action. Whilst your hand is
enjoying itself, and giving your lover the
greatest delight also, his hand will be
stirring up the very depths of pleasure in
you. By the way, before I forget it, let me
warn you, when handling a man's prick in
this way, do not caress its head too much.
It is excessively sensitive, and too much
rubbing produces spams, very delicious for
him, but destructive of your pleasure, for
you might make it too excited, and cause
him to be too ready to spend. The longer
a man takes during the fuck the greater
your pleasure, for he does not spend over

and over again during a fuck, but once only. That done, he is done, too, for the time. So confine your caresses to the shaft of his prick, to his balls, his groins, and his bush, but leave the head of his prick alone, if you are wise Whilst you are thus caressing him, he will be kissing you. He will be squeezing your dear little bubbies. He will be toying with your tongue with the tip of his. Presently his mouth will kiss you along your neck, until it reaches your bosom. He will kiss your breast with rapture, and nibble each little hard rosebud. Whilst sending your wild in this manner, his hand will glide over your smooth body and seek your motte; you will feel his hand press between your thighs. Then he will stroke your cunnie so "—she did it to me—" he will gently press the lips of your cunt together, and tickle your clitoris, this little kind of tongue, a veritable imitation of his own prick, but much smaller, then he will slip his big middle finger deep into your cunnie, and tickle you here."

She slipped hers in and found the narrow,

tight, inner entrance, which she set on fire immediately with her caressing, making me involuntarily spend.

"You quick little darling!" she exclaimed, "how you do spend! won't you just like being fucked? Well, now I must not use you up in that way. Keep your spend for bye and bye, when we will have another bout of rub-cunnie. Now, Susan," she continued, again taking possession of my glowing bubbies, "you can feel, even from my poor little feminine hand, how very sensitive your cunt is all about the entrance. It is sensitive all along its whole depth, but the sensitive portion *par excellence* is about the entrance. The difference between a good fucker and an indifferent one, is in the fact that the really good fucker knows this and does his best to produce the most ecstatic pleasure in you, by cultivating this extra sensitiveness of the entrance to your cunnie. Suppose your man now with his two knees between yours. He leans over, but not upon you He supports himself on his elbow. You take his prick, and plant its head justly and neatly between the lips of your cunnie. Then you put your arms round his waist, and with a little pressure on his part in goes his prick, quite over the shoulder of its head. Its hood slips back, and you feel the sweet thing filling the outer vestibule of your cunt. Then he draws back until he is almost out, and again smoothly and gently pushes in again. This time, with an indescribable thrill, you feel that big head force its way sweetly past the inner, narrow entrance. That thrill is worth a fortune! it is so delicious. Then he draws back again until he is almost out again; with more decided sweeps he thrusts his powerful swelling prick in, passes the narrows, and buries it half way in your throbbing and beating cunnie. These movements he continues, always drawing almost out, always gaining, by gentle but smoothly repeated thrusts, ground in your cunt. Presently, and all too quickly, you feel his pendant balls touch you beneath your cunnie Then they beat more firmly against you, and last of all his belly, which has been touching yours all along, presses yours; his hairy motte mingles its brush with yours; your cushion feels his, and his last trust brings your bodies into the most intimate and close contact. Now the real delight begins. Every stroke, every thrust he gives, is from head to heel of his prick. He gives you long, smooth, deliberate thrusts; every line of those long seven or eight inches tells upon you. You come, you spend, time after time, yet not a drop goes outside. His prick, so to say, closes your cunnie tightly, and your spend only makes its movements more easy inside you. As your pleasure increases, so does his. Presently his agonies of delight begin. All his nerves seem concentrated in the head of his prick, until his sensations are so vivid as almost to take his senses away. Then begin the all too short, as time is concerned, short digs. He shortens his strokes, but quickens them, banging his balls against you with great force. Then suddenly he spends, he pours out the fullest riches of his manly strength. You feel it flowing fast into you, like a torrent, like a powerful artery shooting its blood into you. He presses you as though he would crush you into pulp. He forces his prick in, even further than you would think possible. Your downy motte is flattened by his, and all Heaven and its Glories seem open to you! It is over. You have been fucked, and well fucked, then comes a delightful interval of repose. He lets his body lie all along yours, and he kisses you, and pets you, and calls you all the pretty things he thinks of. His manly bosom rests on your heaving bubbies, your cunnie, if it has the nutcrackers, tightens and loosens on his prick, giving him further delight. Your motte throbs against his, until you become conscious that his prick does not fill you quite so much as it did, and you feel it gradually slipping out. Your lover gets from between your thighs, and lies on his side, clasping you with his arms, and locking his thighs with yours, as mine do now. The fuck is at an end, and cannot be repeated until his prick stands again."

"What are the nutcrackers, Lucia?" said I gasping for breath. My heart was in my throat with the emotion her description had raised."

"The nutcrackers, darling," said she, "are when your cunnie grasps his prick, as it were, like this," she continued, taking my wrist in her hand, and clasping it at intervals of time with her forefinger and thumb. "It must be the muscles about the narrow entrance that do it, for my lovers always tell me that they feel the tightening of my cunt about two inches up from their balls, and only there."

"I say! Lucia!"

"What, darling?"

"Do you know by what geographical expression our cunts ought to be called."

"No. What do you mean? said Lucia, laughing.

"Why, the Red Sea to be sure! Just inside the lips should be the Gulf of Aden, where it is pretty wide; the narrows should be the Bad-el-Mandeb Straits; and the rest the Red Sea."

" Capital! darling! I'll tell **Gladys,** who will laugh, I know. Now," she continued, stroking my cunnie in a lively manner, " now, open your thighs again, my own sweetest darling, dear Susan, and let me have you again."

Nothing loth I did so, and soon **Lucia** was thrilling both herself and me with the pleasure her up and down strokes gave to each of us. At last she made me so tremendously excited that I could lie quiet no longer I clasped her to my belly with all my might, and as her cunnie swept down over mine, I gave a vigorous push up with mine. The result was delicious. Both Lucia and I gave went to a little cry of pleasure, for it so happened that her stiff little clitoris had just reached mine, and my push up made these delicate, charmingly sensitive, little organs penetrate, slightly indeed, but still penetrate, our respective cunnies. The immedi e consequence was copious spendings on either side Lucia kissed me frantically, grave up the sweeping movement, and pushed her cunt straight at mine. Our clitorises rubbed in a most ravishing manner, writhed and thrust, and thrust and writhed, and spent time after time, until fairly exhausted, and the perspiration standing in little pearls on our foreheads, we relaxed our hold on one another, and Lucia, resuming her place by my side, lay panting, but quiet. At length she said :—

" How Nature *does* teach, Susan ! "

" Yes dear," said I, still struggling for breath, " but how? "

" But how? " she cried, " Listen to her. But how? Why, what made you give such a delicious buck, darling? It had not entered my head to tell you. I never did it with any girl, myself, and would not have believed it could have been of any use had it been proposed. What made you do it? "

" Do you mean why did I push up? "

" Yes, why did you buck, as pushing up is called? "

" Buck rhymes with fuck, does it not, Lucia? "

" Of course, and cunt with hunt, prick

with lick, balls with halls, bush with push, and so on, but what has that to do with your bucking, Susan? "

' I can't tell you, darling," said I kissing her, " I only know I could not lie quiet any longer, and so I gave a buck up, like a horse does when his rider spurs him too much."

" Well, Susan! I can only say that if ever a girl was created for the purpose of fucking, you are she. You seem to take to it like a babe does to its mother's breast. Ah! I do envy the fellows who will have you. I know right well they will think your cunt Heaven."

" I don't know, Lucia! they may not like it at all."

" Oh! won't they? A man likes a girl to show that he gives her pleasure. They don't like buck-jumping horses, but they do love a good bucking girl, and you do it as if you had been trained to it."

" Well, no one trained me, Lucia, as you know, for I did not imagine any pleasure, such as you have given me, was ever to be extracted from my cunnie. But do you buck when a man is fucking you? "

" Oh yes! but there is an art in it."

" How? "

" Well, you see, the object of bucking is to get in the very last quarter-inch of the fellow's prick, which would probably remain outside if you did not buck; to get a good strain on to his balls; to get a good squeeze together of your two mottes. All that adds to the pleasure of both of you. The time to buck, is when you feel his balls begin to touch you, then begin a gentle upward stroke, or perhaps a kind of circular stroke, ending with a good bump against his motte. If you begin too soon, you hurry his stroke, a thing to be avoided, because you make him spend too soon; the buck should, as I say, be so scientifically done as to complete the entire swallowing up of his prick in your cunnie! "

" I see. Now tell me, Lucia, if I have learnt the lesson right. When a man fucks you, he ought to get his prick in little by little? "

"Just so!"

"Then, after he has once got it in the whole way, he should draw it all but out, and then with one long sweeping stroke, bring it right up to his balls?"

"Right up to his motte, darling, for his balls touch you first."

"Ah, yes! right up to his motte. Then he should go on so, until he begins to feel that he can no longer withhold his spend, and then he is to fuck like fury."

"Just so—like fury," repeated Lucia, laughing, and kissing me.

"Well then! should I buck like fury too?"

"No; because, unless you kept exact time, you might throw him off his stroke. The best way, then, is to raise your hips as much as possible, and, so to say, give him your cunt more freely than ever. When you feel him spending, clasp your thighs round him. Press him to your bubbies and belly, bite and kiss him, and let him feel that you are as much in heaven as he is.'

"Ah! I see!"

" There is another thing you might do which is not bad. When you feel him spending, shake him well, by alternately and quickly drawing up each foot and thrusting it out straight again. Get on to me and I will show you how, darling! "

I got between Lucia's thighs. I pressed my cunnie to hers. I could not resist giving her some strokes with mine, our mutual fury recommenced, but the roles were altered. At first Lucia responded to my thrusts by vigorous pushes; at last she held me tight, so that our cunts exactly covered one another, and our clitorises were side by side, and then, drawing up one knee, she suddenly straightened it again, at the same time drawing up the other and again straightening it. This she continued until we were simply smothered with spend. It was exquisite, our cunts seemed to open and swallow one another, our clitorises rubbed against one another, and when we left off, we found it impossible to lie in such a wet bed. We got up, washed our cunnies, our mottes, and thighs, and then we walked, naked as we were, to her room, where we got into her cool, clean, dry bed, leaving mine to dry as best it could Then Lucia said :—

" Susan, darling! there is only one serious drawing to fucking, and that is its extreme danger!"

" Danger! " I echoed, " what danger, Lucia? "

" Babies! " she said

" Babies! "

" Yes, babies! You see, darling, when a man spends in us, he shoots into us enough stuff to make thousands of babies, if, like fishes, we were capable of producing thousands of eggs at one time."

" Eggs! Lucia! What are you talking of? "

" Facts! Susan! solid, sober facts, of which I must tell you too, and which you must remember, and be well on your guard always

" Oh, Lucia! " I cried, " Is that really true? Don't humbug me, darling! If there is one thing I have longed to know about, it is how babies are born. I, of course, could not be so entirely ignorant, but that I knew that a baby proceeds from its mother. The Bible tells us that much. I guessed, too, that something mysterious happened between husband and wife whereby a baby was manufactured, but I had really no idea of fucking! I had no idea that my cunnie was anything more than an accident of nature. The truth is, that since you have taught me these exquisite pleasures, the real facts have begun to dawn upon me; but even now I am ignorant of why fucking should produce babies, and you astonish me still more by speaking of eggs! Are women hens, then? When do they lay eggs? tell me! I am dying to know, if only from a scientific point of view. Tell me, darling!" and I kissed Lucia again and again, as if to coax her to tell me a secret she was really quite as anxious to impart to me, as I was to hear it; only, in my eagerness, I forgot that one who had been so free from all restraint both of action and word with me would not be like my mother, who used to tell me I was too young to understand, whenever I approached her as to this thorny, or perhaps I might more appropriately say this 'prickly,' subject of creation."

Lucia laughed at my eagerness.

"Ah, Susan!" she cried, clasping me in her arms, and kissing me so kindly, "I can see that it is more from a desire to learn the matter as a science, than to know how to protect your sweet little belly from swelling, that you are so eager about it. Well, darling; though my most particular desire is to teach you how to defend yourself from the deadly effects of an unprotected fuck, however nice it may be at the time, yet, as you wish it, I will give you the history of your womb and ovaries, of what they produce; and of the spend of a man, and what it produces, scientifically, as a doctor, for I know the subject well, having often and often talked it over with doctors, fucking friends, lovers of mine. Don't interrupt me more than you can help, and I will tell you exactly, point by point, what the process is.

You know already in theory, and soon, I hope, will know it also by practice, what fucking is—that sweetest, most ravishing of all delights. Fucking is only a means to an end. The real end, in nature, is procreation. Fucking causes the male to part with his fertilising spend. It is wrong to call it ' seed,' for the seed is really in the woman, not in the man. The man fertilises it, just as your bees and insects fertilise flowers by shaking the pollen on to the stamens. In every flower there is a cunt, darling."

" A cunt! " I cried.

" Yes, dearest, a regular sweet smelling, beautiful cunt. But most plants have hermaphrodite flowers—*i.e.*, blossoms which contain both the male and the female organs of reproduction. Of these plants, some, however, have male flowers and female flowers quite separate from one another. The bees and other insects go from flower to flower. They accidentally gather pollen from one, and carry it to another. Some of the pollen shaken off them on to the stamens of the second flower, the impregnation takes place—the flower,—the pretty cunt withers, the petals fall off, but the seed swells, ripens, and in time is fit for sowing again "

" But surely a girl's cunt does not wither like that, Lucia ? "

" No, darling," she said, laughing and stroking mine with her taper slender fingers. " Our cunts don't wither, but they certainly are not improved by child bearing. They lose their freshness, and when you consider how much, how greatly they must be expanded by a child, however small, being forced into the world through them, you can imagine such a thing happening as permanent enlargement. But any increase in size —$i.e.$, diameter,—materially affects the pleasure of subsequent fucks, and I know that men complain of this enlargement of their wive's cunts. Some get bigger than others; but undoubtedly the best fucks are given by cunts which have never granted a passage of a child into the world. However, I am digressing."

"Oh! not at all, Lucia! This is most interesting. To think that a rose, for instance, is only another form of a cunt! Oh! fancy talking of a nosegay as a bunch of cunts!"

And I laughed.

"Just so! it is quite true, Susan, and when a gentleman gives you a moss-rose, it is a very direct allusion to your cunt, darling. The flower is the cunt, the moss the bush which grows about it. So if you wore a moss-rose in your bosom, and gave it to a gentleman who is up to sniff, he will at once remember the sweet little mossy cunt, which lies so snug and warm between your lovely thighs."

"Ah! that is the language of flowers. I see it. Now I know why a moss rose means love."

"Just so. Because a woman surrenders her cunt as the gift of love to the man she loves. But we are far from our point, Susan. Let us return to our subject Men have a pair of balls, as you now know. From these balls proceeds, by a roundabout road, the so-called seed, which, deposited in our cunts, produces babies. But we girls, too, have a pair of balls."

"Balls! Girls have balls, Lucia?"

"Yes, darling, but inside, deep, somewhere near the backbone. These balls are called ovaries. Once a month a ripe girl has a flow of blood, as it were. It is at this time she is producing *eggs*."

"*Eggs!*"

"Yes, *eggs!* very small indeed, not bigger than a pin's head, but real *eggs* all the same. There is a tube leading from each ovary to the top of the womb, and down these tubes the *eggs* travel. It is still a question whether the *eggs* reach the womb fertilised, or whether they are fertilised in the womb, but that is a question for science to unravel. Our question is, how to prevent them being fertilised? Well, now listen. The womb is an organ about the size of a medium big pear. It is pear-shaped. Its broadest part is highest, the stalk end, as it were, enters our cunts, or vaginas, as doctors call them, at the top.

a small hole in the communication between the womb and the cunt. This hole is very tightly closed, but tight as it is, it can allow the spermatozoids to pass, and there are little filaments, like hairs, extremely small indeed, lining this hole, which continually work, sucking up all they can get to come from the cunt. Well! a man's spend literally swarms with spermatozoids. Hush! I'll tell you what they are, but give me time. They are little microscopic objects, something like tadpoles in shape, having a head and a long (for them) tail. They swim, and dart, and wriggle about. When a man spends in us, he shoots hundreds of thousands in, which at once dart about in a perfect lake of our spend, corked up in our cunts by the man's big prick. Of course, if the mouth of the womb be left unprotected, all the little reptiles have to do, is to walk up the hole, and get into the womb, helped by the cilia, which I have spoken of as like little hairs. Even if they don't do it at once, they, or some of them, will remain clinging to the lining of our cunts, and in time they will moke for the mouth of the womb and get in. Then somewhere or other, they will meet with our egg, if one is ready. They stick their heads into it, and the mischief is done. The egg is fertilised, and in nine months' time the result will be a fat baby."

"How wonderful! Lucia, you darling! You can't tell how glad, how delighted I am to learn this. Now I understand why, what Martha calls love-children come into the world. I thought that only married women could have babies, yet I know that some unmarried girls had some too, and I wondered how they got them, as they had no husbands. I can't tell you all the absurd ideas I used to have on this subject. I wish I had a book to read all about it in, with pictures, so that I might be sure I thoroughly understood it all. It would give me great delight. And to think of those marvellous tadpole things! I suppose, then, that the reason some women never have families must be, either because their husband shoots no tadpoles into them, or they have no eggs ready?"

"Ah! Susan! that is a subject of which I am ignorant, and I don't think doctors even are agreed about it. But I can only tell you that I would never trust to luck, and go without protection from probable evil results, when I have a man. As to eggs not being ready, why, the worst is that these horrible little tadpoles only ask for a snug warm moist place to live in, and there they will remain alive; so that, as the egg is bound to come sooner or later in a healthy woman, the tadpole is equally bound to get at it. Say that one of my lovers was here now, and first fucked me, and then fucked you, first one each· it is now ten or twelve days since I had my monthlies, when did you last have yours?"

"Last week, darling."

"Very well. You would almost certainly have a baby this day nine months. I might escape, but only if the tapoles in me all perished, from herhaps want of some ailment, which a man has, but I have not, but if a tadpole, one only, happened to live until I next was ill, I too should have a baby, a few days after yours. Oh! fucking is heavenly; but it is terribly dangerous, when the wedding-ring does not make it the right thing in the eyes of the world."

" But Lucia," I said, an uneasy feeling coming over me, making all the life seem to leave my hitherto hot little cunt, " if fucking be so terribly dangerous, how is it you care to run such fearful risks? I should imagine that fear would take almost all the sense of pleasure away. I know I should think of nothing but the tadpoles. I don't think I will let any man fuck me, now I have heard what you have told me."

" Oh! dear, yes, you will, Susan," cried Lucia, laughing. " I am glad I have scared you so well, because you must always bear in mind what I have told you, that, unless you are fully protected, you can't have a more dangerous thing in you than a man's prick."

" But how do you get this protection, Lucia?" I asked anxiously, " and how have you escaped? To hear you, one would imagine that you do hardly anything else than fuck, and you appear to have a perfect armoury of pricks and balls at your disposal."

"So I have, darling," said Lucia, kissing me, and reviving my crestfallen cunnie with her soothing hand. "I should have to reckon all my lovers, and it would take more than the fingers on your two hands and the toes on your feet, and mine too, to be able to count all the darling pricks that have been up my cunnie, and as to the number of times they have given me the full delight, I really could not, at the moment, tell you, though I have all recorded at home, names, dates, numbers of fucks and all. But then I protected myself. It is extremely easy."

"But how? But how?" I cried.

"Well! all one has to do, is to prevent the tadpoles from getting into our womb, and that can be easily done by means of a piece of sponge."

"Sponge!"

"Yes, sponge! Look, I will show you my constant campanion," and she jumped out of bed, and her lovely white nakedness shone in the light of the candles, as she walked to her chest of drawers. She took a little ivory box from off it, and returned towards me.

How lovely she looked. Her elegant figure, her round polished shoulders, her beautiful limbs, her broad gracefully shaped hips, and the brilliant whiteness of her belly and thighs, brought out vividly by the rich dark thick bush which covered her swelling motte, whilst her exquisite rosy-tipped bubbies stood out firm, like those of a statue in marble, all flashed on me, and were all enhanced by the natural elegance of her movements. Oh! I felt that were I a man, I should forget all about possible danger to her, and should desire of all things to clasp that lovely body to mine, and thrust my fervent burning prick in, up to my balls, in the sweet little cunt I could see half hidden under the dark brown hair, in its snug retreat between her beautiful thighs Should I then, when naked, before a man equally naked, forget my danger in his manly beauty. Suppose instead of being a girl, Lucia had been a handsome youth? Suppose, instead of that lovely pounting little cunt before my eyes, I saw a pair of splendid balls, surmounted by a magnificent big, big, big prick, all stiff and standing, such as she had described, would I not be very likely to forget that all that splendour covered a deep danger? That those glorious pendants might originate irretrievable disaster, and that prick, so handsome, so alluring, so desire-compelling, might leave behind it unutterable woe, if I admitted it within my burning and randy little cunt. I felt grateful then to Lucia, that before any such terrible temptations to indulge my passions were likely to assail me, she had opened my eyes to the sense of danger, but I resolved to do as she said, to indulge myself, so soon as I found the lover, and so soon as I quite knew all about the protection, of which she had so eloquently praised the merits. These thoughts flashed through me in a much, much shorter time than it has taken me to jot them down, sweet girl-reader Ah! dear girl, read these pages attentively, and profit by the experience you will gain. Then lie with your lover, then fuck with your lover, gain all the pleasures, and avoid all the dangers of fruitful, delicious love!

Lucia sat on the bed, and unscrewing the top of the ivory box, drew out of it a fat little glass bottle, having a wide mouth securely fastened with a ground glass-stopper. Putting in her taper finger, she fished up a little ivory bar, in the centre of which was fastened a rose-coloured silken thread. This she pulled out until it lifted up a sponge of very fine texture, about as big as a large walnut The sponge was full of moisture, which she squeezed out into the bottle, and then she held it out to me.

" See! " she said " This sponge, Susan, is my shield and buckler! When I am going to fuck, I first put it into my cunnie, so,' doing it as she spoke; "I push it in with my finger as far as I can, and my lover rams it home with his stiff prick When it is home it covers the mouth of my womb, and when my lover spends, it comes between my womb and his prick. No spend can possibly pass through it, and even if any did, the tadpoles would be all killed by the liquid with which this sponge is filled. It is a mixture of carbonised oil, glycerine and a little rose water to give it a pleasant smell. The carbonic acid, small though it be in quantity, is sufficient for the purpose, and no tadpole can stand its effects. Well! this little piece of ivory prevents the up-and down-movements of my lover's prick from rucking up the cord, and pushing it, too, up the top of my cunnie; and after every fuck I make it the practice, not only to pull out the sponge, which of course brings out most of my lover's spend, and mine too with it, but I syringe my cunnie well with a mixture of the same lotion as was in the sponge and soft, warm water Every atom of spend must thus be removed, and I can't possibly run any danger. The syringeing, if done soon enough, would do equally well; but then good-bye to the delicious quiet lying with the sweet prick in me, because, my womb being unprotected, a tadpole *might, even in that short time,* get in! also good-bye *al fresco* fucks, in the green fields, or in the train, or in a drawing-room, or anywhere, where it would be impossible to use a syringe; unless, indeed, my lover had any letters about him. But I dont' like letters. I like a naked prick. I always fancy I feel the dead skin of the letter when my lovers use them."

" What do you mean by *letters*, Lucia ? "

" Oh! they are not real letters. I do not know why they are so called, Susan; but they are little coverings of skin, or thin indiarubber, which men put on their pricks, and which either fit them thight, being elastic, or are tied close to their balls with little ribbons. Then, of course, not a drop of spend can get into me, because it is all caught by the letter."

" But that seems very convenient."

" Well, it is! but I prefer my sponge, which is quite as safe, and does not interpose itself between my lover's prick and the lining of my cunt."

" And what is the syringe like, Lucia? Is it like those gardeners use?"

" Bless you, no! girl! It is—but I have one! Ah! happy thought, I have some warm water here; we will syringe our cunts out now! Jump up, dear!"

I did so. Lucia put the basin on the floor, and getting a tumbler, she filled it with warm water. Then she got a long box, about eight inches, by two wide, and two deep. Out of this she took a long flexible tube, about eighteen inches long, with an ivory nozzle, and also, in the middle, a kind of large bellows swelling. To the ivory nozzle she fixed another slightly curved, but rigid tube, rounded at the end and pierced there with holes. This passed through a piece of polished ebony, or stiff leather, shaped like an oval, and big enough to quite cover a cunt, which indeed was the object of it. Seating herself over the basin, she put one end of the tube into the tumbler of water, whilst she passed the rigid end right up her cunnie, until the shield came over its lips : holding the shield tightly against her cunt, she began to squeeze the bulb in the centre of the flexible tube, and soon I saw that the water in the tumbler was diminishing rapidly in quantity.

"Are you pumping that water into your cunt, Lucia?" I asked.

"Yes, darling, and it fills it deliciously."

"There!" she said, relaxing her pressure on the shield, upon which the water rushed out of her cunt into the basin with a splash, "there! that was very refreshing! Come, and let me syringe you, darling!"

"But," said I, "herhaps that won't go up me, Lucia! Remember I have still my maidenhead! No lover has cleared that obstacle away in me, as yours have in you."

"Oh, that won't matter. You would have to have a very, very fine maidenhead to prevent this passing, and, as a matter of fact, I have felt my finger go past it."

She caught me round the waist, and put her middle finger up my cunt as she spoke, until her knuckles touched its lips.

"There! I can feel your maidenhead plainly, Susan. The tip of my finger is a good inch past it. Don't you feel me pressing at it?"

"I do," said I.

After this I made no further objection. The tube gave me a delightful sensation as it passed up. I held the shield firmly pressed against me. Lucia renewed the water, and worked the syringe. It was delicious! The water quite filled me inside and I had a kind of foretaste of what it must feel like, when one's cunt is filled by a fine voluminous prick!

Having dried our mottes, Lucia put away her syringe and sponge, and then we returned to bed, but she asked me to let her have a good long look at my cunnie, which, she said, was such a perfect jewel she wished to examine it thoroughly. To be able to do this with ease, she asked me to lie down on my back, across the bed, so that my legs might hang down over the side. I did so. Then, she fell to admiring my feet, ankles, calves, knees, and thighs,

kissing them all, as her wanton eyes wa[n]
dered to regions higher still. It w[as]
exquisite, all these warm and almost pa[s]
sionate kisses!

"Now! Susan darling! put one leg o[ver]
each of my shoulders. Ah, that is it. N[ow]
I have this sweet little cunt of yours in f[ull]
view! Lie still, darling, whilst I examine [it]
to my entire satisfaction, in all its beauti[ful]
details!"

I lay quiet as a mouse. I felt her ar[ms]
encircle my thighs, and her hands approa[ch]
my motte, the long curling bush of wh[ich]
she stroked, and then her fingers, separ[at]
ing and parting the hairs which crossed [the]
soft entrance to my cunnie. These delic[ate]
little touches gave me infinite pleasure. [It]
seemed as though Lucia delighted in givi[ng]
me fresh and fresher experience. Presen[tly]
I felt her press her thumbs gently so as [to]
open the top of my cunt.

"Oh! the sweet, sweet, little ruby c[li]
toris!" she cried: "Oh! Susan, you ha[ve]
such a pretty, pretty little tongue here. [I]
really must kiss it!" and down went [her]
hot lips on to my cunt.

I cried out: " Ah! Lucia! don't do that, darling. That is not nice."

" Not nice! " cried she, raising her head. " Do you mean, Susan dearest, that I hurt you; that my kisses there are unpleasant to you? "

" No, darling, but surely it is not a nice thing to put one's lips on such a part of the body as that."

" Oh! " said she, " Is that all? Now darling, I like to do it to you, and I like it done to myself, and I strongly suspect when you have had a little more of it you will like it extremely. Just see if you won't! "

Down went her lascivious mouth on to my cunt again. Really and truly I had liked it there the moment I felt what the sensation was like. I had only cried out because I felt the small stock of modesty I had left repugnant to such an action. However, as Lucia said she liked doing it, I did not mind, and I lay still.

But only for a moment, for Lucia having seized my stiff little clitoris between her lips, began to mouth it, and to touch it smartly with her tongue, in so ravishing a manner, that I could not help crying out with the excessive pleasure she gave me. I did not resist, but I could not lie still. I moved under her devouring mouth, driven half frantic with the powerful sensations of exquisite, almost painful delight she gave me. Lucia seemed prepared for this, for she followed all my movements with skill and patience. If I snatched her electrified prey from between her lips, she instantly seized it again whilst her fingers tickled my motte or groins, or gently plucked at my curling bush. Presently she left my clitoris and ran on the line of my cunt with the tip of her tongue. I felt her face press my motte, her hands smoothly pass on my belly until they reached my bubbies. They took possession of them; my nipples were sweetly squeezed between her fingers, whilst she felt my breasts and magnetised them with her caressing palms. Her cheeks felt so hot against my thighs that they seemed to burn them. But oh! how to express my astonished sensations when I distinctly felt her tongue, gathered as it were into a rod, penetrate deep within my cunnie's lips, and touch the exquisitely sensitive Straits of Bab-el-Mandeb.

"Lucia! Lucia! for God's sake don't do it any more. You are killing me with pleasure. Oh! dear girl! if you don't take care! I'm going to. spend! I'm go..ing to spend! to *spend!* I tell you! oh..h..h.. h..h!" and I felt a flood leave me. It must have inundated Lucia's face, but she only continued her actions, until at last, having spent several times, I acctually managed, by drawing my foot up and planting my toes on a delicious elastic breast, to push her away.

Like a tigress bereft of her prey, Lucia rose, with fire flashing from her eyes, her cheeks red with passion, her bosom shining from the moist offerings I had ejected, and seizing me by the thighs she placed me full length on the bed, and then sprang on top of me. With her knees she opened mine and forcibly spread out my thighs, and then commenced a passionate amorous combat, for which, in truth, I was nothing loth. Our cunts seemed to fit, our clitorises clashed, and seemed to penetrate deeper than they had yet done. Our mottes got drenched with our mutual spend. I twisted, I wriggled, I fought valiantly, and played my part to perfection, for I was maddened with the almost supernatural excess of voluptuous feelings this lovely burning Sapho inspired me with. At length, after a struggle prolonged until nature seemed to become exhausted, Lucia lay motionless, but panting, on my belly, until we had both somewhat recovered our lost breath. Then, still lying between my thighs, Lucia raised her head, and looked inexpressible love, and kissing me with rapture, gently rubbing her bubbies crossways with mine, she said :

" There! Susan! I have no more to teach you of the pleasure one girl can take with another. Some women even prefer such delights to those which man can give them. I don't share their opinions, but after you have learnt what it is to be well fucked you must tell me."

"Oh! Lucia! I can't tell! Perhaps I may after all find a sweet cunt like yours better even than a fine prick."

"Well! I don't think so," said she, laughing. "But it is getting late, my pet. Come, let us go to your room. Your bed is probably dry by this, and mine, look at it! swamped."

And so it was. We rose, washed our cunts, and bushes, and thighs, once more, and went to my room. Our modest chemises once again disappeared from sight under our nightdresses, through which the little hills of our bosoms made themselves very apparent, and then we got into my bed, and locking one another in our arms we soon fell fast asleep.

I dare say my reader will say, that it was wonderful how an innocent girl like myself could have been so quickly converted into a perfect Lesbian. But, dear reader, if of the male sex, do you remember how quickly you learnt to love when the fair woman, who first taught you what your prick was for, took it, and pressed it in the velvet palms of her hands? After that first powerful appeal to your passions, how long did ignorance prevail over knowledge? Did you remain shy and coy? or did you plunge at once into that delightful vortex of voluptuous passion? I know your reply, you need not answer. And you, oh! sweet girl when your eager lover first passed a passionate hand under your petticoats, and, seizing the lovely prey of your ardent little cunt, glided a tempting finger into its hot depths, did not that sweet cunt beg you to listen to his prayers, and having once been ravished of your modest maidenhead, and having felt the rapture of that stalwart prick, the soft pressure of those pleasant-feeling balls, and the inexpressible poesy of the movements of the blissful fuck, tell me, did you hesitate to open your thighs a second, a third, nay, a thousandth time to your nasty lover? " Ce n'est que le premier pas qui coûte," after that the progress is rapid. Once the spark has been set to the combustibles, the fire rages. So it was with me. Lucia had suddenly attacked me by the weakest side; without knowing or thinking I yielded, and my readers will see if I have ever had reason to regret commencing a course of pleasure which has made my life up to this one continual feast, one endless song of happy delight.

THE TADPOLES, ETC.

We slept long and soundly after our exploits of the night, and it was already near noon before either of us awoke. Lucia cried out, when, on looking at my watch, she saw what the time was, and without waiting to give me any more caresses, she fled to her room, bidding me at the same time to be quick with my toilet

On going downstairs Martha met me in the breakfast room, and looked all astonishment.

"My goodness, child," said she, "what ever makes you so late this morning?

went to see why you were not up It gave me quite a turn when you did not come down at your usual hour. I could not but think of your poor dear papa, who died in his sleep. But when I saw you and Miss Lucia sleeping so calmly in one another's arms, and saw by your bosoms rising and falling that it was only natural sleep, I left off being frightened Ah! you did look a pretty pair. I could have wished, though, instead of Miss Lucia, I had seen a handsome young husband in your bed, who on waking would have given his pretty bird a sweet wakening, as young active husbands always wake their wives "

As she was saying these last few words Lucia came into the room

" What was that you were saying, Mrs. Warmart, about young husbands waking their wives? " said she.

" I was just telling Miss Susan how I wished you had been her young man, Miss, when I saw the two of you so fast asleep this morning when I went to call her, and I was a-saying that if you had been, you would have waked her in a way she would have dearly liked."

"Ah! true enough. So I would, and I can tell you, Mrs Warmart, that when I saw how nicely Susan is made, I wished I was a young man myself last night, twenty times "

"Ah! well! young ladies!" replied Martha, laughing, but still sufficiently seriously, " you must not let your imaginations run away too much with you. Young men are not to be trusted, remember; and temptation comes very often when one is least on one's guard, and what is pleasure at first often ends in pain at last."

"Yes, Mrs. Warmart, that I believe is true enough! But now have you any breakfast for us? I am hungry enough to feel that I could gobble up Susan, and if I let my hunger get the better of me I would make a complete end of her, which is more than the young man would do."

Martha laughed and quickly put our breakfast on the table. Lucia and I, famished with our long fast, gladly fell to, and we both ate heartily.

" Ah! now I feel better, Susan. How do you feel this morning? None the worse, I hope, for our delicious tête-a-tête last night? "

" All the better, I think," said I, " only I feel rather stretched in the thigh joints."

" So do I," said Lucia, " now; that comes from want of practice. It is such an age since I opened my thighs to anyone! "

" However," she continued, " it won't be long, I hope, before I shall have lots more practice than way; and my lovely Susan begin hers. Oh! Susan! how I almost envy you, to know for the first time what a man is."

I laughed.

" Look, darling! " Lucia ran on, " I want to write a letter to Gladys, and to do one or two little things for myself, so I'll just run up to my room. You won't mind my leaving you for a little while, will you?"

" No dear! " I said, " I will go and feed my little pets and gather some flowers ..."

"And dream of young men!" laughed Lucia

"Very likely," said I, "especially when I have gathered a bunch of cunts."

"You darling!" exclaimed Lucia, kissing me in her boisterous manner, "You deserve a most luscious fucking, you come so quick in mind and body," and pressing me once more in her arms, and kissing me again, she ran off

Often and often have I wondered how I never seemed to see an inkling of that moral haven, which I have so often read of, as being the immediate result of following the natural bent of one's desires. I so often read, and have so often heard *good* people say that the inevitable result of "sinning" (and in the eyes of 999 out of 1,000 *good* women fucking with anyone not one's husband is sin—hardly anything else being so) was miserable repentance, and a wretched state of one's conscience. With me it has been just the reverse. I admit I have been fortunate, in so far that my acts have not been productive of unhappy results. I have no doubt we all regret having done anything, which produces unfortunate consequences either for ourselves or for others, but such acts may not necessarily be *sins*. I don't know that a married woman enjoys her husband any the more because what he does to her in bed is " lawful and right." I fancy a prick is a prick, and a cunt a cunt, whether the conjunction of them be " lawful " or " unlawful." All I know is, that whether the prick be that of a married or of an unmarried man it makes no difference to me, so long as it be a good one, and well wielded; and my cunt seems naturally formed to receive pricks, and all I can say is, that those of men who are gentle in idea and behaviour are ever welcome to it, and afford it and me such pleasure that I never say " no," unless prudential reasons cause me, with a sigh, to decline the delightful offering. I don't know what the current of my thoughts was that morning, but I imagine I was looking forward to those halcyon days when, according to Lucia, I should have the voluptuous delight of knowing, from vivid experience, what it felt like to have a handsome and vigorous man stretched at full length between my glowing thighs, delighting me with his caresses!

When I came in an hour later, Lucia was still upstairs, and I sat down with a book in my hand, but my mind still running on the pleasures I had so lately learnt.

After a while Lucia came downstairs, dressed ready for a walk, and holding a sketching block in her hand.

"Come, Susan dear," she said, "we breakfasted so late that I think neither of us could eat any lunch Let us go out for a ramble over the fields We will take some biscuits in our pockets, and I may show you some sketches I made. Perhaps if I can find a pretty view I may make a sketch this afternoon."

"All right, Lucia!" I cried, and running upstairs, I quickly put on my hat and light jacket, and joined Lucia down in the breakfast-room

We sallied forth, having first told Mrs.

Warmart we might not be in again for some hours.

"Ah! that's right, Miss Lucia!" said the old dame, looking at my sweet cousin with beaming face and smiles; "you are the right sort! I do believe that if you had not come here, poor Miss Susan would be sitting indoors now, moping to death."

"Susan!" said Lucia, as we made our way along the path, "do you know one of the things you should carefully cultivate is exercise, good outdoor exercise? and walking is one of the best, because it is the least fatiguing, whilst at the same time it calls into play every muscle of your body. A good walker always carries himself upright: he gets good square shoulders, and a fine projecting chest, and he is always in good trim. It adds firmness to the flesh, and tone to the body, and a girl who wishes to preserve a good figure, to have fine breasts, firm, round and delightful to see and feel, can't do better than take plenty of walking exercise, in the fields if possible. Beside. the mere healthiness of the walk, there is another and not unimportant result. Now although, as I explained last night, the sponge and syringe are perfect safeguards against the insidious approach to our wombs of the active spermatozoa, yet, if it be possible to still further defend ourselves, we should be foolish not to do it Now, without being in the least degree uncharitable towards my neighbours, who in public denounce what they call illicit intercourse with men as sinful and wicked, yet my own experience has shown me that a very great number of ladies, both married and unmarried, have their lovers, whilst I know that numbers of shopgirls and servant maids have theirs also, and I do not think I am at at all overshooting the mark when I say that at least one half of them, shopgirls and servant maids, have their lovers at least once a week, if not oftener.

"But, as hardly any of them use any precaution whatever, if should follow that half the nubile women should, whether married or not, be always in the family way, whereas the truth is that this is not so, and why? Well! most of the girls of whom I speak are obliged to have their fucks either in the fields, or in some hidden corner, not in bed, and so soon as Master Johnnie Prick is out of their cunnies, the girls spring to their feet, and more often so as not to attract attention should any chance passenger come by "

" The consequence is that the seed has a tendency to run out of their little cunts. This I believe to be the reason why servants and shopgirls so frequently escape being impregnated.

" But take young married couples. Now I think you may be sure that during the honeymoon fucking is the constant action which goes on By rights, then, every young married woman should have a baby in nine months from the time she first went to bed with her husband The facts, however, are against this theory. It is so comparatively rare for a baby to appear so punctually that when one does keep such excellent time, the husband gets clapped the back, as if he must be a splendid former, a perfect stallion, a grand bull, whereas, if the truth were known, his wife is rather a lazy young person, who prefers lying on the sofa to going out for a walk! By and bye, you will, when in society, have opportunities of observing the truth of what I say—viz., that the active young wives who walk are much longer free from pregnancy than those who do not walk, and that the worst thing a girl, who wishes to become a mother, can do, is to be active on her feet, or on horseback! Consequently, girls who, like myself, have no right husbands, but dozens of ardent, strong-backed lovers, can't do better than take plenty of exercise, either on foot or on horseback, as it is an additional safeguard from having a swelling and inconvenient belly!"

I listened quietly to those words of wisdom, and I strongly recommend my dear girl readers to mark them too, and to put in practice the sound advice of my dear cousin Lucia. For, however delightful fucking may be. there are people who could not stand in the light of day if the results are to be an increase of the population, and you, dear unmarried girls, are of that number. Having at length arrived in a field of several acres extent, with high hedges all round, and trees dotted here and there, Lucia said she thought we might rest under one of the trees, and she would show me her sketches. She chose a spot some distance from the path, and the moment she produced her water-colour drawings from the pocket of her sketch-block, I saw why she had gone so far from where any chance passer-by might see her pretty pictures, or hear our conversation!

My breath was almost taken away, when the first she put into my hand represented a fine and handsome young man, perfectly *naked!*

Everything was there! The picture was perfect! It was beautifully done, and was a portrait! I could recognise the features of the handsome, manly face of my cousin Charlie Althair; but I did not scan those features so eagerly as I did certain others, half-way between his chin and his feet. For there I saw most beautifully delineated the charms, *the* charms, which affect woman most powerfully. The moment Lucia had chosen to represent, was when Charlie was not in that state in which his .adyloves most liked to find him; in other words, he was in a state of complete repose. Lucia had drawn his bush perfectly, and out of the lower portion of it grew that sweet, sweet chubby prick, reposing on a pair of well rounded, tightly closed-up balls. I could see at once that it was an exact representation, though I had never seen the real object of which I had the portrait before me. I felt my cheeks crimson, and my stays grew so tight on my bosom that I felt choking.

Lucia said nothing. She very quietly watched my increasing agitation until I turned my burning eyes on her face.

" Well! Susan! That is Charlie Althair in puris naturalibus! What do you think of him? "

" Oh! Lucia! and did you do this yourself? "

" Yes, dear. But it was difficult enough to get Charlie as quiet as that," and she laid the point of her pretty finger on his prick, " that article, when I am near, is generally in this condition," and she slid another sketch over the first one in my hands.

" Oh! my! " On gazing on this second work of undoubted art and skill I could not resist giving vent to a cry of admiration and wonder. For there, in all its glorious might, power, and beauty, was what I presumed was the same prick, but erect, grand, swollen, big, and certainly as stiff as if carved out of living flesh-coloured marble. Its curious, wonderful-looking head was uncovered, and for the first time I quite understood the vivid description Lucia had given me of this beautiful member, the night before. How I studied it! How my cunt burnt and throbbed at the sight! I could feel my breasts swell, their nipples grow hard, and my clitoris stand. I was forced to put my hand between my thighs, and Lucia, delighted, gently pushed me on my back, and looking carefully round to be sure no uncalled-for intruder was near, she quickly slipped her hand under my petticoats, found my beating cunnie, and gently insinuated a spend-provoking, but most grateful finger deep between its burning lips.

Whilst she thus imitated the movements, I held before me the delicious object her pleasant finger represented to me very palpably. Oh! let the day soon come when, instead of a girl's finger, this glorious prick might invade my longing cunt, and feel on my rounded haunches the weight of those splendid balls. I could have lain so for an indefinite time, but Lucia, always careful, said the place was too open, and that such exquisite sports were better deferred until we could safely indulge in them where, by no possibility, prying eyes might see us at play. Reluctantly I resumed my sitting position, and Lucia replaced my petticoats, but my faithful Spot came sniffing, and Lucia laughingly lifted my dress for him, saying that no doubt his tongue would be as clever as her finger. Good dear Spot! the first male being that ever kissed my cunnie. How grateful to your loving mistress was your soft hot tongue that afternoon! Picture after picture did Lucia show me, most of them illustrative of amorous couples indulging in the joys of erotic bliss. Drawn by the hand of one who fully sympathised with all she had delineated, and by a hand evidently possessing marvellous skill and dexterity; these pictures were really gems of art.

Nothing could more powerfully appeal to the passions than these lovely living representations did, and had Lucia doubted my perfect willingness to embark on a career of Paphian exploits, she could not have possibly hit upon a better method for convincing a hesitating mind. My mind, however, required no further encouragement than it had already received from her words. These voluptuous actions, transferred in all their naked beauty to the papers I held in my hands, only tended to increase the eager desire I had to take my part in the most delicious and exhilirating of all pursuits Again and again I looked them over, I begged for more and more, until Lucia wisely said that my colour was so like that of a peony, we must really continue our walk, until my cheeks had resumed the natural rosy tints which usually adorned them So Spot was relieved of a duty he had apparently relished, and one he had marvellously well performed, for though I had spent perfect floods the faithful dog had allowed none to run to waste

" Oh! Lucia! " I said, as we continued our walk, " when shall I be able to go with you to Sunning Hill? For I am to go with you, darling, am I not? You would not leave me here to mope after you had gone?"

" Of course you shall come with me, darling Susan! " she cried, " but so much depends upon old Penwick. I think we must hurry the old gentleman up. We will go and see him in his office to-morrow when we go to Worcester."

"And does Gladys know I am coming with you, you darling, dearest Lucia?"

"Oh yes But until she gets my letter, which I sent to post this morning, she won't know that our snug Nunnery is to have another lovely novice. We won't go to Sunning Hill, Susan! we shall go to London, where I am badly wanted; read this" and she gave me a letter, evidently written by a lady from the character of the writing. It ran thus :

"Dearest Lucia,—When are you coming back. When will you be able to leave our little country cousin, and return to the disconsolate swains who, poor fellows, we are obliged to tell that they cannot be accomodated because our loveliest girl is away. I hope you are not playing fox, and that all this while you are enjoying the pleasures of love with foxhunting squires, grave country curates, or handsome young farmers? What is Susan like? Has she any penchant for our naughty ways? Have you sounded her? Do you think, supposing she is pretty enough—and she should be, as she is of our same blood, a blood which has never produced an ugly child yet —she could be induced to give up her chance of a single husband for the certainty of a plurality of much more interesting and ever fresh lovers? To be plain, do you think she will fuck, if the chance be offered her of doing so without fear of evil consequences? Of course, unless she is naturally inclined to do so, I don't advocate her coming as a nun, and just now it would be awkward to have her as a guest, for never have I known so busy a season. Our guests are numerous, and not a bed unoccupied from one end of the week to the other. If those beds could speak they would tell us some pretty stories. I believe adultery is greatly on the increase, and some of our ladies have more than one lover apiece. Poor Annette and I are, however, really to be either greatly pitied or immensely envied. I don't know which, for sometimes I feel as if my back were broken, I get such a lot of it."

" Not one single night for the last three

weeks in bed alone, and a fresh man every night, not the same man twice in a week. It is the same with Annette.

"My usual time will be next week, and there will be only Annette. So do, for goodness, come if only to pay a flying visit, but come and relieve us for that week, otherwise I fear our disappointed lovers may fly to fields not so wholesome as ours. Bring your own dear little cunt to the rescue, and if possible bring Susan's also."

"Charlie Althair says he has not had a real good night since he last had you. I believe he has adorned his prick with one or two more maidenheads whilst you were away.

"He loves tender virgins, and makes them love him! Adieu, darling Lucia! I am to have Sir Thomas Gordon to-night. You may remember I had him about eighteen months ago at his mother's house.

"Your poor loving cousin,

"GLADYS"

"Well," said Lucia, as I handed back the letter to her, "what do you think I told Gladys in my reply this morning?"

"I suppose you said that you thought I would go with you, dear."

"Yes! indeed I did! and I said more, I told her that you, were absolutely beautiful from the crown of your head to the soles of your feet, and that your disposition was so amorous, your temperament so ardent, that you would be the very finest possible acquisition I told her that I had found you, darling, in a state of extraordinary simplicity and ignorance, but that the moment I reflected from the mirror of my mind and experience the ways of enlightening knowledge, you had spread out not only your lovely rounded bosom, but your exquisitely chiselled thighs to receive all I had to give you, and that so plentiful was the will of love, between the aforesaid voluptuous thighs, that it hardly asked to be touched before it overflowed with the offerings of sympathy, and that though the sweet cunnie sheltered by its lovely bush, was virgin of virgin, yet I knew that short as had been the period since it had first been excited to mobility, it would gladly accept the sacrifice of its peerless maidenhead, and admit the stalwart prick of that happy lover who, alone of men born of women, will have the delicious privilege of carrying the light of knowledge to its hottest dephts, I——"

" Oh! enough! enough," I cried laughingly, putting up my hand to stop her torrent of words, " I am deli~hted you told Gladys all this, and oh! Lucia! I do long! I do long for that perfect knowledge which you have so eloquently described."

" And your longing shall soon, very soon be indulged," cried Lucia, " oh! we must hurry up old Penwick, and perhaps with n a week my Susan shall have had not only one, but twenty, thirty, forty good, solid, succulent fucks! "

I bounded on, leaping and running, so great was my excitement. Never, never was girl more madly happy than I to hear this, and yet hardly twenty-four hours had elapsed since, to all intents and purposes, my now raging cunt was dead asleep. Oh! how wide awake it was now!

I asked Lucia to let me read Gladys's letter once more. It interested me, but I did not understand the whole of it.

" What does she mean by our guests, Lucia ? "

" Oh, they are people, ladies and gentlemen, chiefly married ladies, who wishing for change of diet, long for flesh pots they don't find in their husbands' beds—in other words married ladies who fall in love with other men. They find it difficult to indulge their very natural passions in their own houses, still more difficult to do so in the houses of their lovers, and are afraid to go to hotels for fear of being recognised by other visitors there. We know so many people in high society that we know those whom we can trust, and there are ladies amongst our friends who sympathise with the anguish of lovers panting to enjoy a good fuck, and we permit our house to be named as a safe Bower of Bliss, where snug rooms, and comfortable beds, and perfect incognito can be found. We get a note, say a day or two before the happy night, fixed upon for the full enjoyment; Gladys or I meet the lady, as it were by accident, at our friend's house, the matter is quietly arranged. We ask the lady to dinner, she gets another invitation from our mutual friend to a quiet ladies' party at her house, she accepts the latter, tells her husband she is going there, but comes to us instead. Her beau, if we don't know him at first, comes to our house at dinner-time, merely mentions the name fixed on which his lady is to bear in our house, and is admitted as a matter of course. We sometimes sit down to dinner a party of eighteen or twenty; five of the twenty may be my lover, Gladys's, Annette's, Gladys, and I, the remainder would be seven couples who come to enjoy a sweet half or whole night in one another's embraces, and the odd are either a guest, a lady friend, or a gentleman for whom we can't provide a bed and a cunt."

"And do these different couples know that the others are also going to fuck, Lucia?"

"Not unless they have intimate acquaintance with one another. Our rule is, that when at table, or in the drawing-room, only the manners of society as it exists are to rule—*i.e.*, there must be no amorous talk or play. A stranger would have no idea that anything more than a social meeting was intended, and I can assure you our reunions are delightful, as every-one is in a state of excitement more or less subdued, and all are expecting a delicious time in a few short hours. You will see that about 10 o'clock, as the time goes, people will rise to go away. Gladys will press them to give her the pleasure of their company for a little longer. They will excuse themselves, but as they leave the room they go upstairs instead of down; and after the ladies have had a few minutes' grace, to arrange such little matters as they would not care to settle in the presence of their lovers, the gentlemen follow, discreetly kept from treading on one another's heels by either myself, Gladys, or Annette, who keep them in conversation until the coast is clear, when a gentle good night and pressure of the hand tells them they can safety go to the rooms where their respective ladies are undressing and preparing to receive them."

"So in that way, I suppose, you prevent one gentleman seeing where another goes?"

"Quite so; not only that, but we are so clever that no gentleman sees another go upstairs at all."

"And how do they know their rooms, because if they are strangers to the house, and there are so many bedrooms, how can they avoid making a mistake?"

"That is very simple. We tell their ladies to give them the hint at dinner. In each guest's wineglass is put a flower different to any other in the room: say one is a carnation, another a rose, another a lily or what you like. When the gentleman goes upstairs, he looks for a door having his flower in the keyhole, he opens the door, walks in, and there is his lady, more or less undressed. Nothing can be more simple or well contrived, my dear Susan."

" But surely they must notice that every keyhole has a flower in it! and would not that make them suspect that others were on the same errand as themselves? "

" Oh, my darling Susan, you may be sure that men and women of the world have an immense amount of discretion, and don't see more than is needful. No doubt they do see *a lot*, but they say nothing, and, as a matter of fact, every-body minds his own affairs. We never have any trouble. Our guests must be well recommended, or else they would get no invitations, and the recommendations we get come from the highest quarters! "

" But! " I persisted, as idea after idea presented itself to my mind, " it must put you to a lot of expense, all these dinners and entertainments."

" So it does! " replied Lucia, with gentle acquiescence; " but Gladys is rich, so am I, and even if we wished it we cannot prevent very handsome presents being made us, not only by our own lovers, but by those who reap the advantage of acquaintance with us:

all goes to help, but our motives are not mercenary—we live the merriest, most delightful of lives, and what we do is from a love of pleasure. You see, we have no object on which to spend the seven or eight thousand a year we have between us, and so we can afford to be generous to Love. As it is, we do not spend half our income."

"Ah, that explains it all," I said; "but tell me, Lucia, who is Annette, whom you mentioned just now?"

"She is our confidential maid, a most lovely girl, whom a young Henry Pendleton seduced; she was his sister's maid I took his maidenhead, he continued by taking Annette's; but unfortunately his mamma found her in his bed, and turned her out of doors then and there. Her parents, being strict Presbyterians, would not take her back, and she would have gone on the streets as a last resort, or drowned herself, had not poor Henry, in a state of unguish, for he is a dear, kind hearted boy, written and implored me to help Annette. I sent for and saw her. Her exceeding beauty at once recommended her to me, and I took her on as my own maid. Little by little I found she was as amorous as a pigeon, and I proposed to her to admit a lover of mine, whom I could not take because another had a pre-engagement with me one night. She was delighted, and I heard such an excellent report of her next morning that I took her on as my Aide-de-Con! "

" Aide-de-*Camp!* " said I. " Lucia, you don't pronounce it properly! "

" Don't I, dear? Well, I tkink I do! *Con* is the French for *cunt*, and I say truly when I say that Annette is my Aide-de-*Con!* "

I laughed, and was delighted at this new kind of staff appointment!

" So, I suppose, I am an *Aide-de-Con* that is to be, Lucia? "

" Of course, darling, if you like to look on it that way; but I hope you will always remember that, whereas by her agreement Annette must take any man we give her, you come to fuck, or not, as you please.

You are, and will be, entirely your own mistress in that respect. We shall introduce gentlemen to you, and it is for *you* to introduce them or not, as you please, into your charming little cunt!"

"Oh, I don't think I shall raise many objections," said I, laughing.

"Nor does Annette! She is as lewd and lascivious as I am, and that is saying a good deal, my Susan!"

In this delightful manner we wandered on, chatting and laughing, and picturing all kinds of lovely events, when our conversation turned once more on the danger of *unprotected fucking*, a subject Lucia was extremely anxious to bring well home to my mind, and when once more she commenced holding forth about those most interesting but dangerous little atomies, tadpoles in the spend of a man, I said to her:—

"Lucia, you talk as if you had actually seen the horrid little things!"

"So I have!"

"How?"

"Through a microscope, darling!"

" But how? When ? "

" I will tell you," said she. " But here is a nice shady place. Sit down, and try and don't grow so red as you did over the picture of Charlie Althair's prick ! "

" Oh, do let me see those pictures again ! I can listen whilst you tell me all about the tadpoles! "

" Most appropriately, too, Susan! for it was from Charlie Althair's balls that they come! "

" Was it now really! " I exclaimed, as I once more gazed with extraordinary pleasure on their vivid-looking portraits, " from these dear balls! Oh, how I shall like to see the real articles myself some day! "

" So you will, Susan darling, and soon! Do you know, I have been thinking that as Charlie Althair took my maidenhead, it would be as well if he had yours also, Susan What do you think? Of course you have a perfect right to do with your own what you like, and, may be, you might prefer some other man than Charlie to do that pleasant job for you You have only to say frankly what you wish It would be easy to have a half-dozen handsome young bucks for you to make your choice from.

"Oh! Lucia!" I said, feeling half suffocated as the reality of the nearness of what I now most longed for became more and more apparent, " I don't think I can hesitate It is true I don't know my cousin Charlie very well; still, I have seen him, and he has kissed me, when I was a little girl and he was growing up into a young man. I think we should look upon this as a family matter, and settle it in the family; so I think I'll give Charlie my maidenhead, if he thinks it worth the plucking!

"If he thinks it worth the plucking!" exclaimed Lucia "My dearest Susan, if we only had time, I should say, let Charlie beg and implore on his knees for such a priceless boon, as the granting him a fuck at all! but it is imperatively necessary, if you are to join us, that you should commence operations at once, and as, before any real work can be done, your maidenhead must go, I say let Charlie have it. He is a dear, nice fellow, a splendid bedfellow, and I don't know any man I could better recommend to you, darling!"

"Very well, then that is settled, Lucia. But do tell me now about how you saw the tadpoles!"

"Well!" she said, "about eighteen months ago, that is some time in the early spring of last year, Charlie came to see us in Park Lane, where we had gone to prepare for the London season Frank Holt, the famous portrait painter, had just finished my picture, and we had invited him and a few of our most intimate and trusted friends to see it. Charlie had written to say he was afraid he could not come then, as he had an engagement in the country; in fact, as usual, he was after a virgin, and was fast bringing her to hear reason, and he could not afford to leave her just when he was apparently on the point of victory. Now, Charlie is one of the very best hearted fellows going There is a girl, a clergyman's daughter, Clara Doobs, whom he had induced to take him between her thighs some twelve months previously, a fine handsome creature, very spirited, amorous, passionately fond of fucking; a girl in fact, whom we all like, and who, when she heard of the advantages of our society, required no pressure to make her join it *con amore*. It was easy for people in our position to make the acquaintance of her father and mother, down in Buckinghamshire, and they, good simple folk, were easily induced to let Clara visit her rich and fashionable London friends We have had her father and mother up, too, to stay with us with Clara, and that, too, at times when we might have seven or eight beds occupied by amorous couples, *one of them having Clara herself in it with Charlie Althair or some other fine young fellow*, and you may judge how extremely well everything went off, and how well we manage things, when our guests, the Dobbs, old people, never smelt a rat, and imagined the house was fast asleep, whilst the most lively performances.

in which their own daughter was playing her part, were going on! "

" But, Lucia! what has this to do with the tadpoles, dear? "

" Now, Susan! have patience; you must always let me tell my story in my own way "

" I beg your pardon, darling! I won't interrupt again—it is really most interesting. You are very, very clever people."

" Well! as I said before, it was Charlie who first taught Clara how to fuck, and gave her that taste for it which will never fade as long as her cunnie retains its lively powers. He was exceedingly proud of having gained this maidenhead, because Clara had been really very strictly brought up, was old enough to know all about the relations of the sexes, and was in fact not at all a girl to be surprised by her senses into any false step. It took Charlie nearly three months of the most careful and assiduous attention to bring her to see the joy she might have if she admitted him to her bed, but at last she did, and it was in her own father's house that Charlie assailed her lovely cunt, and took the maidenhead she had guarded so well. From that day, or night rather, Clara never lost an opportunity of being fucked. Charlie took care of her, taught her all that was needful to know, so as to keep herself safe, but as she, at first, had no man but him, she had no necessity to guard herself. Charlie did that for her. However, after she joined us, and became an associate, she fucked very freely with all the men we introduced to her. Amongst these is Allan Mac-Allan, a great huge Highlander, a magnificent man, a great bull, a regular satisfying Hercules, especially what we woman like to find, a man big and powerful. But unfortunately Allan is selfish in so far, that, so long as he gets what he wants, he is not very particular in looking after the satefy of the woman he has been having, in regard to the chances of her being exposed to have a baby. We therefore always cautioned Clara against him, but naturally, like all of us, she liked so fine a man as Allan, and would always choose him for her bedfellow, even before Charlie, if she had the chance. Now you know enough to understand what is going to follow.

" Well, to our surprise then, Charlie turned up early, that is, about lunchtime of the day we were giving our little rout in honour of my portrait being finished. We had arranged our party so that none but our most intimate and trusted friends should be there, all were to be associates, and there was to be a very delightful night spent in worshipping Venus. Consequently we had no girl for Charlie, unless we took Annette's man from her, and this we did not like to do. We told Charlie how sorry we were, and blew him up for not letting us know in time that he was coming, when we could so easily have had a nice sweet little cunt for him, and then we asked him if he had been successful, and scored the maidenhead he was in chase of. He laughed, and thanked us, and said the maidenhead was still as intact as ever, as far as he knew, and that for the present he had to drop the pursuit, but that he hoped to take it up again very soon. Then he said —' Oh! dear girls! I am sure you will be very much grieved to hear it, but Clara Dobbs is in the family way ' ' Oh! no! oh! no! ' we screamed! ' How can that be? Are you certain, Charlie?' ' I'm as sure as can be, I am as certain of it as I am that I have had both of you, Gladys and Lucia; as certain of it as that I took Clara's maidenhead.' We were most dreadfully shocked. This is how Charlie told us. He said .—' I was to have added another maidenhead to my list, the night before last, everything was prepared, Julia Lawrence had consented at last and was eager to give it to me, when I got these letters. The first ran —

"' Dear Mr. Althair,—Papa and mamma desire me to ask you to come and dine and stay the night here, unless your engagements prevent you You are to be scolded for coming to our part of the country without making our house your home. It was quite by accident that we learnt that you are staying at the Swan. Mamma begs me to say she hopes you will not disappoint us. With papa's and mamma's kind regards.

"'Believe me, yours truly,
"'CLARA DOBBS.'

"Enclosed in this was another letter, which was couched in these words.

"'Dearest Charlie,—Believe me, I would not beseech and pray you to come and spend the night with me, knowing as I do how near you are getting the prize you have so long been striving after, only that it is a matter of life and death with me. I have most fearful news to tell you, and it can't be delayed. I entreat you, dearest Charlie, to remember that I gave myself to you before you ever knew Julia, and by the maidenhead which you reaped then I beseech you to come to your most unhappy, unfortunate Clara.'

"Well," said Charlie, "If Clara had not had heaps of fellows after me, I should have thought it was jealousy on her part; if she had not, herself, helped me to fuck other girls than herself, I should have refused to listen to her A fellow can't very easily tell a maiden, who has at last consented to have him, that he can't conveniently do it then, and I was at my wit's ends to know what to say. Julia was to be at the Swan that evening with her people, who did not, and were not to know that I was there, but everything was cut and dried, the head chambermaid was my ally, and everything would have gone well; I should have had a night of delight in Julia's arms but for this unhappy letter I therefore returned at once, whilst there was time, to London, to send myself a telegram, saying my mother was extremely ill, and supposed to be dying, and then returned to the Swan, got my telegram, put it in a despairing note for Julia, which I gave to the chambermaid to give her on her arrival, and then I drove to the Rectory I have not yet heard how Julia took the news, but I am certain she must have spent a most unhappy night.

"The Dobbs were awfully glad to see me, and easily accepted my excuses for not calling on them. Clara looked beautiful and radiant as ever, and I could see no sign of the frightful woe which, according to her letter, she ought to have been in, as it was a matter of life and death with her, and I declare it took all my powers of self-control to prevent my showing how desperately disinclined I was to stay in the house. The hour when Julia was to be at the hotel was dreadful to me when it came, and to think that she was within a quarter of a mile from me, and that all I had to do was to walk over, wait a little, and find myself, at 11 o'clock that night, between thighs which I burned to lie between, and enjoying a sweet and lovely cunt, which no man but I had as yet even felt with his hand, or fucked with his finger; her darling little maidenhead seemed to pull at the finger which had felt it, as much as to say : ' I am here! come and pluck me,' and I heard the soft amorous voice again saying to me. we shall be at the Swan on the 13th of this month, come then and you shall have me if you don't change your mind between this and then.' God! it was awful! yet I bore it all! At last bedtime came Clara pressed my hand and whispered ' in an hour, and that hour, I, of course, had to wait, turning about on my bed until it would be quite safe to go to her. Dear girls, I suffered agony of mind and body, thinking of Julia in her bed, and no chance of going to her. I almost doubted Clara. I thought it might only be a trick, and I vowed if it was I would leave her and go off to the Swan, if I had to risk dropping 20 feet from my window to the ground to get out of the house. But when the time came for saying good night, Clara had pressed my hand, and said in a low tone, ' come to my room in an hour when all is quiet. I have something dreadful to tell you,' and the light and youthful expression which had been in her face all the evening up to this departed, her eyes grew dark and mournful, and her mouth expressed a dangerous tendency to sobbing I had returned her pressure with an ' I will,' and she went upstairs. Of course I knew that, whatever it might be that Clara was about to tell me, I should be most of the night in her bed, and that she would expect me to fuck her, so I undressed, and when all was quiet, I went to Clara's room. She was not in bed. She was undressed and in her night shift, and the moment I entered and had shut the door, she ran to me and clasped me in her arms, and pressing me to her bosom, burst into an agony of weeping, which alarmed me so much that my prick ceased to be stiff, but hung at half cock.

" ' What is the matter, Clara dear?' said I, ' come, tell me! '

" ' Oh! Charlie! she said. ' It is too dreadful, and I know you will blame me. But indeed, I could not help it!

" ' But what is it, Clara?

" She cried, she sobbed. She clasped me with desperate energy Her lovely bubbies pressed my bosom and excited me. Up went my prick again, but the point of it seemed to me to strike her belly further in than it usually did on such occasions. I put down my hand to help it up, so as to get it between her belly and mine, and give it a sweet squeeze between us, when the cause of poor Clara's grief and despair instantly betrayed itself! That charming belly was, oh! much too rounded and full

"'Oh! Clara! I cried, 'are you in pod?'

"Yes, yes, Charlie! oh, what am I to do? What am I to do?

"'What brute put you in this state, Clara?' said I, feeling her big belly, whilst, strange to say, my prick grew stiffer and stiffer, as though the idea of a baby being inside the girl made her cunt all the most desirable!

"'Oh! I am sure it was Allan Mac-Allan! I could not at first think who it was, I have had so many men, but I remembered that the last time Allan fucked me he had postponed using the sponge! He was too lazy to get it. We had had a grand night, as usual, and after our last ablution he had put my sponge on the mantelpiece, and then we went to sleep. In the morning when we woke he had m again, but would neither get the sponge nor let me and oh' Charlie, he is such a grand poke! I half believed him when he said that after such a lot of spend as he had given me overnight, he would not have much left. Alas, he *had!* His last spends (and he fucked me three times before we got up) were quite as plentiful as his first. Oh! fool that I was not to have got up at once after the first fuck, but it was so delicious to be in bed with him, that I entirely forget prudence, and here is the result! I am certain it was Allan!'

"'But Clara!" said I, 'you may be mistaken. You may not be really in the family way!'

"'Oh, I know I am! Charlie, I am six months gone, and I can feel the baby kicking inside me' Here, give me your hand. Do you feel that?' I did! Oh, there was no doubt at all! A fine, vigorous baby was at that moment plunging inside his unfortunate mother, and I could feel all his movements, which were dreadfully lively.

Poor Clara! I made her go to bed, and

I got in with her. She let me see her belly, which was much bigger than I had ever seen before, and it looked as if its beautiful white skin was all stretched and polished from excessive fulness Her breasts, too, looked changed. She made no objection to my fucking her Indeed, she said she was only too glad to have me, as it might be the last time she would ever know rapture again. I almost forgot Julia! I don't think I ever enjoyed Clara so much before, and she said she had never felt so full of desire, or so sensitive to the pleasure my prick gave her, as that night. During the intervals we formed all kinds of desperate plans, but, alas! always, when we seemed to be at the point of finding one feasible, by which she might escape, an unthought-of obstacle always reared its poisonous head. All she gained from me was a night of rea good fucking, but I left her as much in despair as ever And now, girls, every day is precious! There is no time to be lost. What is Clara to do?

" We were nonplussed, Gladys and I

Never had such a dire misfortune oc
before. We could only chatter, we
not all at once hit on a plan. Glady:
has more quiet good sense than I hav
she would invite a doctor, friend of l
come and sleep with her, and would c
him during the interval, and then ou
versation fell upon the dangerous ta
which live in the balls of men. V
read of them, but we had never seen
and were saying we would like to se
they were like, when Charlie's eye fe
microscope on the drawing-room
'Girls!' he cried, 'Nothing can be
easy than to show you the tadpoles.
is, if that microscope is powerful er
He jumped up, and took the glass
from off it, put in a slide, looked at
exclaimed that it would do.

" ' Now! ' said he, carefully liftu
instrument, ' Let us go into your f
Lucio, and you shall make me spend
will show you the tadpoles.'

' Both Gladys and I were as ex«
could be; we had had the microscope

time, but the idea of utilising it in this way had never struck us before, we knew all about spermatazoa, theoretically, and we knew how to protect our wombs from the pestilent little objects, but we had never thought of trying to see with our eyes what they were like I know I clapped my hands, and at the same time the idea of the whole thing made me feel more than randy. My cunt jumped and leaped, and Gladys called out at the redness of my cheeks Charlie led the way—he knew my foutoir well Oh! had he not fucked me there often enough? Frank Holt was to have me for the first time, that night, there also, as a reward for painting my portrait Oh! Susan! he must paint you too. You should see what a lovely picture he will make, and mind! he will give you your bush and cunt as large and as plain as life! "

" When Charlie saw the picture of me hanging over the mantelpiece he laid down the microscope, and exclaimed at the beauty of it. Frank has made me as a girl going for her morning bath in a clear stream. I am first looking round, as I throw off my robe, and I am in the act of coming down some steps which lead through tall reeds under the shade of a tree to the limpid water. The spectator's eye is supposed to be on a level with my knees, so that he can, by just looking up, see all those beauties which lie between my thighs. Charlie was in raptures. It was the best painted cunt he said he had ever seen, and turning to me he said, ' Lucia, let us compare the original with the portrait ! ' ' All right,' said I, laughing, ' But I don't believe Frank Holt has idealised at all,' and I at once commenced undressing. ' Wait! ' cried Gladys. ' It would be as well that Annette saw the tadpoles too. I will ring for her! ' ' Well ! said Charlie, now I tell you what ! Let us have a quartette. Gladys, you strip too! Annette will also ; so will I, and we will have a sacrifice in honour of science, which the very gods will appreciate.' I clapped my hands, for I saw what must be the inevitable result, and Gladys in her quiet way get three sponges ready. You may be sure Annette made no opposition, and very soon there we were, all four, as naked as we were born. Charlie said the picture was certainly lovely, but that it had not, to his idea, done me full justice, and that my real flesh and blood cunt was worth fifty of its portraits in oil or water colour. Then we arranged how to make Charlie spend, for, of course, it would not do for him to lose it in any of our cunts. At first Gladys proposed he should fuck each of us, taking care not to spend in any of us, but when he felt himself coming, to snatch himself out of the cunt he might be in at the moment, but Charlie himself said 'No!' He said when once he got near the short digs he must continue, and he could not withdraw from a cunt which was giving him rapture even if its owner consented, a thing he greatly doubted. A little thought convinced us of the truth of his remarks. So this was how we managed

" Gladys sat on the ottoman, which is

very large and soft, and with her back supported, opened her thighs wide, so that Charlie might lie back along her belly, with his head on her bubbies and his arms round her thighs He could thus feel her bush somewhere about the middle of his back

" Annette, kneeling between his legs, was to caress his balls, whilst he gazed at her lovely white bosom and its rich and beautiful snowy globes, whilst I, kneeling on one side of him, was to manipulate his splendid prick, with my hand moving up and down, and have a cup ready to catch his spend when it came I declare it was most voluptuous Oh! Susan! how you *will* like feeling a splendid prick! I worked Charlie's with all the voluptuous ardour I could command He seemed to think it delicious He soon gave up looking at anything. He half shut his eyes, and his parted lips showed how great his pleasure was. Suddenly he called out : 'Quick! Quicker! Lucia!' I hastened my movements; my hand flew up and down his prick! and, with a burst, the torrent of creamy spend shot up like a fountain, falling in its first jet upon Gladys's bosom, in its second on to Charlie's, and then, each jet getting less and less strong, it finally poured all hot and scalding over my hand! and I had quite forgotten to try and catch any in the cup!

" For a few seconds we all remained as still as statues. I was amazed at the quantity of spend which had come from Charlie. and also the tremendous force with which he had ejaculated it and I fancy Gladys and Annette were quite as much surprised as I was, for was it not funny, Susan darling, when you come to think of it? Neither of us, not one of us three girls had ever *seen* a man spend before, though we had often seen the spend itself and felt it dashing into us hundreds and hundreds of times! I shall have to tell you something still more funny directly. Well, after a little while. Charlie, who had been lying perfectly still, with his eyes shut and with the most placid expression of complete enjoyment on his face, suddenly looked up and said :—

"'Thank you, Lucia dear. Your little hand is almost as nice and as soft as your sweet little cunt! But I like your cunt bes.'

"Then he looked into the cup, which I still held up in my left hand, for my right was still grasping his grand prick, which was jerking from time to time powerfully, just as I had felt it often when it was in me after a good poke.

"'Why!' he exclaimed; 'you have not got a drop in the cup, Lucia! Where did it all go?'

"'Some on me,' said Gladys in her quiet voice, ' but most on yourself, Charlie dear.'

"Charlie then looked down, and seeing his body all wet, especially his belly and bush, said it did not much matter if none went into the cup, because one drop would be quite sufficient.

"'One drop!' I cried.

"'Yes, one drop!' said Charlie, getting up. 'Oh!' he said, 'Look here! look at Gladys's bush! There is a regular little pool just resting on it, which has not soaked in amongst the hairs yet!'

"And so there was. The first shower Gladys got had been stopped flowing down her body by Charlie's shoulders, but then he got up it had been trickling down between her bubbies, and along her belly, and was like a little pool of cream, looking blueish white, against her coal-black bush!

"Charlie got a slide with a little hollow in it, and a little tube of glass, and picking up a drop of his spend off Gladys, put it on the slide, and then moved to the microscope, through which he looked. After a second or so he called out : ' Come girls! come and see the varmints!' Oh! Susan! I had first look. The drop under the microscope was not so big as an ordinary tear, and yet it was alive with spermatazoa. There they were, hundreds of them, like little grey-coloured tadpoles, head and tail exactly the same, and wriggling about in a way which made me shudder.

"'Now!' said Charlie to me, 'one of

those, if it got into the right place, Lucia, would do your business, and you would have a child! ' "

I, Susan Aked, shuddered when I heard it!

" Oh, Lucia, what terrible dangers you must have run "

" Well, yes, and no Listen After we had all seen the living tadpoles, Charlie proposed to show us those which had been exposed to the liquid in the sponges, and to do that said he had better fuck one of us.

" Gladys said . 'We are all ready, Charlie! you must go the rounds, my dear boy.'

" ' Yes! yes! I cried ; ' have us one after another, Charlie; and what do you say, Gladys, won't it be a good plan if, to make all things equal, Charlie withdraws the moment he makes one of us spend, and then goes to the next, makes her spend, and then the next, makes *her* spend, and then to the first, and so on until he spends himself?

" Annette clapped her hands, and ran to

the ottoman and lay back on it with her lovely thighs—such splendid thighs, Susan—open and ready for Charlie the moment he came.

"Oh! that was such fun. Charlie began with Gladys! Gladys had him for a very few strokes, because she spends very quickly Then he went to Annette, who comes nearly as quickly as Gladys. And last to me; and I got the rapturous short digs: After our thorough enjoyment of the delight of what I may call the afterglow of a luscious fuck, Charlie withdrew his prick, and then getting a slide he gently pulled out my sponge by the thread, when, of course, all the spend in me flowed over it, his and mine mixed together. 'Now!' said he 'come and look at this! As I had been the one most interested I was allowed first peep There they were indeed, the nasty, dangerous little tadpoles, but barely a sign of life in one of them They were all dead as door nails!"

Really and trully?"

Really and truly! Oh! I can tell you,

Susan, we three girls were glad to see it. I do believe we should have been frightened after poor Clara's accident, but for what Charlie showed us. And after each of the other two pokes he gave us, it was just the same, though the liquid in my sponge had not been renewed, for I had the great good luck to be the one in whom Charlie spent each time."

" And you were not frightened ? "

" Oh, not a bit after what I had seen. But oh, Susan, I told you I had never seen a man spend before that day. Well, fancy, I had never seen a man fuck a woman before! It is *such* a fetching sight! The most fetching part is when he is getting the last half-inch or so *in*. The way his hips sink between her thighs, as he presses his motte to hers, is, oh! beyond anything voluptuous in the extreme! Ah! how I did enjoy that afternoon, and indeed I had **good** fun with Frank Holt afterwards! "

" Was he a good poke, Lucia ? "

" Upon my word he was, Susan! He is considerably over fifty, and I never expected more than two grinds from him, and neither of them really good! whereas he gave me six good, solid, real *good* fucks before he slept and one more in the morning! and he knows how to do it, too! He must have been superb when he was young'

" Tell me, Lucia darling! what did you do about poor Clara ? "

" Oh, Gladys slept with her doctor, and after an awful lot of trouble got him to promise to perform an operation on Clara, in our house We invited her up, and Gladys put her under chloroform, so that she might not see who worked upon her poor little quim, and the doctor did it as cleverly as could be The child was born *dead*, and Clara was relieved ; but she was as near dying as could be; such bleeding set in; it took all the doctor knew to stop it, but she was saved, and luckily her parents believed her story about her spraining her ankle, and never came to town to see after her, believing her to be in *such* good hands when she was with us ! She soon got well, and would you believe it, the very first man she had on her recovery was Allan Mac-Allan!

"Oh!"

"Yes! But we gave him such a lecturing that I don't think he will ever 'pooh pooh!' the saviour sponge again."

CHAPTER V

FRUITION

Lucia's story of the tadpoles affected me in more ways than one. I shivered alternately with fright and pleasure. I was something like a person suffering from ague —I had my cold fit succeeded by the hot. At one time I thought that not for all the pleasure in the world would I run the risk of giving admittance to no matter how charming a prick, which would surely leave behind it myriads of these disgusting tadpoles, each one of which constituted a danger of the very greatest importance to me. On the other hand, the fact that Lucia had not hesitated to give herself to Charlie the very minute after he had shown her the nasty wriggling things through the microscope, showed that however great the danger from them might be, she felt convinced that she was so well protected that they could do her no harm, even though she were inundated by an ocean swarming with them. We talked and talked about them until my confidence began to return and I was once more in that state of enraptured expectation that, had Charlie come in, I should not have hesitated to take him between my thighs! Dear reader! I do so regret that I must bring my story to a close just when, in fact, it is only commencing, but I am the victim of circumstances, at the moment necessitating a long journey, and I do not know but that I may be called upon to travel, at all events to shift from place to place, for so long a time that I may not easily find leisure to continue these memoirs, so delightful for me to write and, I trust, pleasant and instructive to read.

Our visit to Worcester took place, and

afforded Lucia an opportunity of dilating upon the handsome cousin who was to be my first lover! We drove past the place where the Althairs used to live, and Lucia pointed out to me where she and Charlie had many a sweet *al fresco*. Oh dear, what a lad Charlie must have been! It was in that house he commenced his career as a lover of women! In that house he committed his first rape! In that house he laid the foundation of his first baby, for the ladies have at times used my cousin Charlie as a stallion when it was their wish to have offspring. And all about Worcester there were sites, sacred to the delicious consummation of love and desire, in which Charlie had been the man, and oh! a great variety of maids and matrons the women! Lucia seemed to have been the repository of all my cousin Charlie's amatory secrets, and her retailing them to me, with all the names of the fair ladies who had surrendered their charms to him. told me more forcibly than anything could how great was the confidence she reposed in me.

I had intended to have made my dear readers acquainted with, at all events, the outlines of these exciting stories, but, alas! I have not the time. I must hurry on, and describe how I put in practice all that Lucia had taught me, and how I surrendered my maidenhead, and learnt the rapture which man, and man alone, can give to woman.

We paid our intended visit to old Penwick, and persuaded him to let me go to London sooner than he had at first thought possible, on the promise that, if I should be required at Worcester, I could return without fail or delay Lucia also ordered some dresses for me.

She got me what she called "decent" drawers, chemises, and stays, and in a very few days we were ready, and started for London.

It was early in August. Few people were travelling to London, that is in the first-class compartments, so that we had our carriage almost entirely to ourselves the whole way

Lucia, expectant of the delight she most prized on earth, was bursting with joy, and radiant with pleasure. We were to have only a "family" party. Allan MacAllan was to be Lucia's man; Sir James Winslow, Gladys's; Robert Dane, Annette's; and Charlie Althair mine. Not for one moment did Lucia leave me to my thoughts; she either by design, or because she really was so excited herself, kept chatting, chatting, chatting to me, and always on the subject of the pleasure, so that, what with her words, and the vivid caresses she continually gave me, I was in a state bordering almost on mania when we at length reached London. Had Charlie met us on the platform he might have taken me into the ladies' waiting room, and had me there and then, and I should have offered not the slightest resistance. Lucia had continued to make me so lewdly randy—there is no other word to express my sensations. My heard and my cunt were on fire, and my blood ran like a torrent of fire through my throbbing veins.

A very handsome carriage and pair driven by a coachman in a splendid livery, and with a footman also, met us at Euston. Lucia spoke kindly and gently to both of the men, who touched their hats, and seemed glad to see her again. I looked keenly at them to see whether anything in their deportment showed that want of respect which, I had been taught to believe, marked the knowledge by men of their mistresses not being all they should be. But I saw nothing but the most well-bred respect, mingled with that affection which all good and well-trained servants show towards employers whom they love. In the state I was in, I could almost have given myself then and there to the footman, for he was a really handsome, well-made young man, and quite fit, as far as personal qualifications were concerned, to lie between a lady's thighs I don't see why a lady may not desire a handsome servant, man, just as gentlemen most certainly desire handsome servant women, so that I do not feel at all ashamed of telling my dear readers of what my feelings were on this occasion.

We drove rapidly though street after street. In spite of my throbbing cunt, and my beating heart, I could not but observe all that I saw, and the huge London, of which I was then seeing but a small portion, struck me with amazement. But the noise prevented much conversation and Lucia made me recline backwards, whilst the only way I knew of how intense her feelings were, was from the repeated hard squeezes she gave my hands.

At length we reached Park Lane, and drew up in front of what, from the outside, seemed so modest looking a house that I was rather disappointed. I had expected to see a more palatial looking building, after all Lucia's descriptions, but I forgot that she had described no more than the inside of the house to me.

A fine well-preserved elderly woman opened the door for us, and once we were inside, Lucia kissed her affectionately

introduced me to her The old lady sh
my hand and said I was a fine, pr
creature.

" Who's at home, Sarah? " asked Lu
" Miss Gladys is upstairs; miss,
Mr Charlie Althair."

My face, I know, became crimson
hearing that name. Then *he, he* who
to—to—oh! **my goodness!** *he* was alre
here!

Yes, indeed. At that moment I saw
lady coming down the stairs followed b
gentleman The lady I guessed to
Gladys, and the gentleman I recognised
be my cousin Charlie, though it was y
since I had last seen him, and he was
a boy then and I a little girl But wh
difference there was in him to wha
recollected! There was a tall, bro
shouldered, strong-looking man, young
deed in face, but a perfect man in form
figure, instead of the slip of a handso
boy as I remembered my cousin Cha
Now he had a fine moustache, and the
looking jaws of a man I think the t

that perhaps struck me most was the appearance of power in him. He looked as if he could pick me up, and put me on his shoulder, and jump with ease over a five-barred gate, and I felt my heart jump with admiration, and I was glad that such a splendid man as he was going to have me. I did not feel a bit shy. Lucia had wound me up to such a pitch that I was shivering with desire, and all the day since we commenced our journey I had had the most extraordinary sensation in the lower part of my body, in the " organs of Love,' first as though millions and millions of ants were creeping and crawling in and out of my cunt, and all over my motte and groins, whilst my breasts seemed to be swollen and itching to be handled and pressed.

Gladys, for it was she, glided—you could not say walked, for her movement was more like that of a stately vessel wafted by a light breeze over smooth water—to Lucia, and the two women embraced one another with hearty hugs and kisses, pressing their breasts together, first on one side, and then on the other. They only said a few words to one another. It was " Well! Gladys!" " Well! Lucia!"

Then they separated, and Lucia flew open-armed to Charlie, and oh! how they kissed and caressed one another! I felt a great pang of jealousy as I saw Lucia's hand fly to the top of Charlie's thighs, move about rapidly as if trying to find something, and at last get it, not at all! where I expected she would have found it, but half-way up to his waist-coat! I felt as jealous as could be of the hot kisses I saw Charlie giving her, and of the joy I knew she must experience feeling his hand stroking her, as it did, between her thighs.

But Gladys, who perhaps noticed the shade on my face, came to me smiling, and gave me oh! such a sweet kiss. What a mouth she had! what lips. It was a kiss which, woman as Gladys was, provoked desire even in me, who was, like her, all but a woman, for before midnight I expected I should be like her no longer a virgin! I returned her embrace with fire My kiss seemed to electrify Gladys, whose thighs locked with mine, and whose hand sought for and pressed my bubbies, and she flushed as she said " Ah! Susan, I see you are just what Lucia said you were! We shall be great friends, darling, I am sure. And how nicely you are made. You have quite a fine bosom, and I dare say, she added with a meaning smile, " you are as well made *here* " (she let her hand fall as low as possible and press against my motte), " and I hope you have brought us an ornament which will be as much admired for its beauty and delightfulness as I am certain your face and figure will be ! " And she kissed me again and again, looked into my eyes with hers, and oh! what eyes she had! They seemed to warm into my very marrow, and to dart torrents of desire and all-voluptuous longings!

Our embraces, caresses, kisses, made me for the moment half forget Charlie and Lucia, for I am a creature of impulse, and if my senses are powerfully affected, as they were at the moment by the sensation of

Gladys's electrifying and really delicious charms, I cannot help yielding up to them What a blessing this is for me! Dear reader, all men are the same to me! Yet that one who holds me in his arms is, for the while, the perfection of mankind! I forget all the others whilst I enjoy his vigour, his manhood, and the rapturous pleasure his exquisite prick gives me.

But if I forgot, or half forgot, Charlie, Lucia did not forget me.

" There! " she said; " that's kissing and roking enough! you two naughty girls! Gladys! Here is Charlie burning to know how his lovely cousin is made! and I am sure Susan would like to make his acquaintance, and that of holy Saint John Thomas, too! "

Gladys laughed, and I felt myself growing red—not with shame, but with the immense pleasure I knew was before me As I quitted the arms of the voluptuous girl, who had been adding fuel to the fire that devoured me, Charlie took me into his.

"How you have grown, Susan!" he said, as he kissed me, keeping his hot lips on my mouth, and passing his still hotter tongue along my lips from corner to corner.

"And so have you, Charlie dear," I answered, as soon as I had the use of my lips to speak.

Charlie held me at arm s length, whilst he looked at me with eager eyes. His two hands held me under the armpits, and whilst he gazed at me as though he had that one chance of doing so and never would again see me and wished to remember me, he gently and gradually brought his hands towards one another in front, and then pressed them on my swelling breasts.

"What good bubbies!" he cried, and then he suddenly turned me round, so that I had my back to him, and pulling my head back against his shoulder, he again snatched the most voluptuous kisses from my mouth and felt first one and then the other of my breasts. Goodness! how different did his strong hand feel to Lucia's, or that of Gladys! Surely some strange influence—perhaps the male influence—passed from his palm into my bubbies, and thence down to my burning cunnie!

I know it was quite different to being handled by Lucia, though, oh! what pleasure she used to give me when she squeezed my bosom with her soft hands!

"Come!" cried Lucia, who had been with Gladys watching all this with eyes dancing with excitement; "come into the study, Charlie! Come, Susan, I want Charlie to assure himself, before me, that I deliver you a perfect maiden into his hands, and that you carry the warranty of your virginity in the pretty cushion between your thighs!"

Charlie put his arm round my waist and urged me towards the door through which Gladys and Lucia had passed, with eager but not unbecoming haste.

There was a large ottoman in this room (there were similar ottomans in every room in the house) and on this Lucia made us sit whilst she and Gladys stood before us.

"Now, first of all, Charlie, you must let me show Susan the Holy Saint who is to say his prayers in the niche prepared for him called her quim!"

Charlie laughed and said — "Certainly"

Lucia with rapid fingers undid his waistcoat, and his braces before and behind; then she unbuttoned his trousers down to the very last button, and, pulling up his shirt, produced what, to my heated imagination, seemed something much larger than I had ever expected to find a man's prick to be. Ah! how different is reality to imagination! I had had Charlie's beautiful prick before me in a picture! I had heard it described! I had formed an idea of its magnitude, bulk, length, and power; but ardent as my imagination had been, minute as Lucia's descriptions had been, the *reality* was vastly more splendid!

"There!" cried Lucia, as she put my hand on to the delicious hot, hard, yet velvety-feeling weapon, round which my eager fingers could hardly meet; "there!

that is the prick which took my maidenhead, Susan! and which will take yours! Oh, beautiful Saint John! oh, glorious Saint John! Is it not *grand*, Susan? Now, is it not as delicious to feel as I told you it would be? But wait until you feel it walking up and down your little silky cunt, my dear Oh! goodness! how I wish I had my first fuck to do again. Now, here! put your hand in and get out the bag of jewels."

I did so I looked at Charlie, who bent his head forward, and as our mouths met, I had his magnificent balls in my hand. Oh! how nice! how extra voluptuous they did feel There is something in the balls of a man which is more fascinating, more captivating than even his glorious prick in all its glory. Is it because his balls are the evidence of his manhood? I can't tell; but I only know that I never tire of feeling a good pair; and I had, at that moment, a splendid, full, hard, big pair of them in my fingers. and could feel them slide from side to side, as I gently pressed them.

"Now, Charlie! Assure yourself of the existence of Susan's maidenhead," and Lucia lifted my dress, petticoats and all, high over my knees.

Charlie needed no hand to guide his to my throbbing cunt. He only held me a little more firmly whils he just pressed his curved hand and finger over my bushy motte and the soft lips of my palpitating quim, and then, putting his tongue deep into my mouth, he slipped his strong middle-finger as far as he could, beetween the full, soft lips of a cunt which, except for Lucia's fingers and twot, had been virgin, since it had been created.

Girls, dears! wait until a lover does the same to you, and then you shall tell me if such caresses are, or are not exquisite!

"Well!" said Lucia, all avidity for Charlie's verdict.

"A perfect virgin," he exclaimed. "A first-class maidenhead. There can be no doubt about that."

"And now has she not a delicious little cunt, Charlie?"

"Awfully good! awfully nice!" was the answer, as his finger gently and sweetly worked up and down, killing me with pleasure.

"Let me feel her maidenhead!" said Gladys, coming forward.

Charlie instantly withdrew his hand, and I saw Gladys give him what looked like a little packet of cigarettes. Then kissing me, she slipped her slender long finger in, and smiling and flushing at the same time, she said :

"Oh, yes! most distinct! a real and true maidenhead! and what a darling little quim. Charlie, I wish you every joy."

"Now, Gladys, I was the original discoverer of this wonderful virginity. So let me have a last feel of it, for I think it won't see the light of another day!" This was Lucia, of course, her hand, oh! that dear little hand which had first made me aware of what immense resources of pleasure were concealed, unknown to me, in that dormant little cunt of mine, took the place of Gladys's.

But all these varying caresses, these different hands, these changing fingers, added to the state of intense excitement in all that highly susceptible region, produced a very natural, but apparently not expected, result. I had Charlie's glorious prick in my grasp again. It alone was capable, even so, of upsetting the equilibrium of my senses, but these fingers moving in and out....

"Oh! you naughty girl, Susan!" exclaimed Lucia, "just look. Gladys, she has spent all over my hand.

"I am very sorry, Lucia Indeed I could not help it," cried I, almost in distress.

"Never mind, darling," they all cried together, and Charlie again taking possession of my quivering cunnie, kissed me really passionately I heard the door shut, and when Charlie gave one a chance of seeing. I found that we were alone. Gladys and Lucia had left the room.

"Susan!" whispered Charlie, in a voice husky with excitement; dear boy, he was always excited, tremendously excited, when on the brink of a nice plump cunt. " Will you, give me your maidenhead now? Ah! say yes! I could not wait till bed-time."

I raised my face and kissed him, and whispered :

" Yes."

With a bound Charlie jumped up. He left me lying across the ottoman.

I heard a quick rustling of clothes, and there he was, with only his shirt and boots and socks on. Whilst I looked at him he tucked his shirt up so that all his body from his waist downwards to the top of his socks was absolutely and perfectly naked. Oh! how I longed to see him as Lucia had drawn him, with nothing on but his skin ; what a handsome object a well made naked man is. How different in every way was he from the slender softness of Lucia. Charlie's muscles seemed like engines of great force, as every movement of his made them play under his white and even skin, and how white his skin did look. I had no

…dea a man's skin could be so white, and it looked all the whiter from the contrast of the dark black hairs which grew in parts wonderfully thick over his body, down the outsides of his thighs and down his legs.

But what naturally attracted my most eager attention was that magnificent, glorious, handsome prick of his. To my astonished vision it appeared to have grown even longer, bigger, and more rigid than ever. It seemed to me, lying down as I was, to reach quite an inch up over his navel, and it was pointing straight up, apparently at his chin. I noticed then the curious shape of the under-side of its well-shaped head, as if it had been carved by nature into two curves meeting near the top, and gracefully sweeping down and asunder, one curve taking the right and the other the left. The shape of that head appeared to make the noble weapon it tipped perfectly irresistible, and I could see how admirably nature had formed it for penetrating. But, oh! could I possibly take in that huge (it did look so huge) thing?

Surely my cunt was neither deep enough, nor wide enough, to admit it all, and, as Lucia had told me, I noticed that it grew broader and broader as it approached its base. I saw too, all along the front, as it appeared to me, a kind of supporting rod under its tight-looking-skin, and of this Lucia had not told me anything that I could remember. And below, hanging in that curiously-wrinkled pouch, which looked as if it had been sewn up all along the middle, were those delicious balls, which I had been feeling. How big they looked, and how beautifully even they seemed to hang, each in its own pocket as it were. And oh! what a splendid bush there was, out of which all these splendours grew. Far thicker and longer and much more curly than either Lucia's or mine.

Charlie saw admiration in my burning and excited glances, and he gave me time to note all, and then when he thought I had seen enough for the present, he said :—

" Now, Susan let me clear *your* decks for action! "

Oh, the swiftness of his hands! He had my dress and petticoats over my face in a trice. He tugged at the band of my drawers, and without mercy burst it. I heard the ripping and felt the tearing, as his powerful fingers tore through the linen, and the fresh feeling of the air on my belly and thighs told me that he had stripped the lower part of my body as naked as his own! I could not see, for my face was covered.

"Susan, darling!" he cried, his voice trembling; "here! look! take this and put it on me."

He handed me a curious-looking little thing, which felt soft and elastic, and had a long deep line in it, for all the world like a little cunt. It was not thicker than an ordinary slate pencil, and about two inches long.

I looked wonderingly at Charlie, for I did not know what I was to do.

"There!" said he, "take hold of me low down, near my balls, with your left hand

That's right. Now lay the letter on the top of my prick. So, only turn the other side (the cunt-shaped side) up Now sweep your hand down, and that thing will open and cover me completely!"

I did exactly what he told me, and lo! there was his prick completely covered almost to its very end with a thin, transparent covering of india-rubber, which looked like another natural skin! This, then, was the covering of which Lucia had told me. I declare if it had not been for seeing this I should never have thought of the dangerous tadpoles! I was so eager, so anxious to be *fucked* that I had altogether forgotten the very serious lessons which dear Lucia had given me.

"Thank you, *dear* Charlie!" I cried. "I know what this is for!"

"Lucia told you, I suppose?"

"Yes! She taught me everything!"

"You could not have a better instructor," said Charlie; "but now, my Susan, for experience!"

"Come!" cried I, lying back and opening my thighs wide, planting my feet firmly on the yielding ottoman.

In another moment Charlie was between them and on me. I felt with a thrill, not to be described for pleasure, as the soft-feeling yet powerful head, separating the lips of my throbbing little cunt, entered! The ease with which it penetrated astonished me. But it was in! in! I could feel it expanding and filling me, as far as it had gone. But something inside me checked it, and Charlie, instead of trying to push it in any further, kept pushing his prick in and out! tickling me in so ravishing a manner that I held my breath to enjoy it the more. All my soul seemed concentrated at that one spot. Little throbs began to shoot all about it, and I knew I was on the point of coming! I expected every moment Charlie would plump deeper in; but he still continued his play, which was on the point of becoming disappointing, when I suddenly came!

Charlie had apparently waited for this, for the moment he perceived it he grasped me to him tighter than ever.

I felt a violent struggle going on. It was the expiring effort of my poor little maidenhead! Then something rent inside me, an extraordinary sensation of neither pain nor pleasure followed, the obstacle was overcome, and with alternate movements backwards and forwards I felt Charlie's prick rapidly gaining ground, and for the first time knew the infinite joy of being filled and stretched to the utmost by the power of man!

"Ah! ah! ah!" cried Charlie at each stroke, and his breath poured hot down my neck inside my collar His balls touched me! I felt them! I bucked! and he was *all* in!

"You *darling!*" he cried, and then began the splendid long strokes

Gods! how nice it was! At first it did not tickle very much The chief pleasure was feeling the alternating filling and contraction of my cunt! but after a few strokes the tickling, from end to end, began to grow more and more brilliant, until it seemed to me that I should faint from the excessive pleasure I experienced! There were perfect spasms, like electric shocks in their force and rapidity, which cannot be described, which, my dear girls, can only be experienced, and with all the most deliciously soothing sensations, indescribably delicious! oh, my God! was it not *Rapture? Rapture* with a very big " *R!* " But alas! the longest fuck is always too short! Charlie's time was come! All of a sudden he commenced those rapid, short digs which sent me wild with an agony of delight! My entire body glowed with the white heat of the glory of heaven! my senses reeled; all the room seemed to whirl round and round. I felt that in another moment I must faint, when, crushing me to him, Charlie for the last time dashed his prick into me to its very furthest limit, and I felt his whole weight on my pimping motte. I felt as if a powerful pump were sending streams in jets against me inside. One, two, three, four, I counted—there were more—but I went into a half-swoon of ecstasy, and seemed to be quite lifted out of all connecting me with earth! I was in a kind of dream in which I saw angels floating around me, *and felt the ineffable blessing of the peace of heaven!*

But Lucia's laughing voice recalled me to earth, and I found myself still in Charlie's arms, and could feel his glorious prick in me, *working*, as if it were trying to burst my quivering cunnie by swelling itself out with repeated efforts

'Well, Susan? Take your head out of the way, Charlie, and let me kiss *my* girl' and I heard a smart slap on my lover's bottom, which vibrated all along his prick and made my cunnie quiver then. "There, there, my own darling Susan!" as she kissed me with impetuous kisses, "not much of a maidenhead left now I fancy Did he hurt you, darling?"

"Hurt! I exclaimed. *Hurt!* oh, how could it hurt me, Lucia dear?"

"Oh, all right," she exclaimed, laughing. "I am glad it did not, but sometimes it does"

"By George Lucia," said Charlie, "I can

tell you it is well Susan has no teeth in her quim, or deuce a bit of a prick would I have left. Oh, if you could only feel her now!"

"Has she the nutcrackers, then?" exclaimed a voice which I knew to be that of Gladys.

"*Has* she? If you were like me, and *in* her, Gladys, you would soon know."

"Oh, Susan, Susan, you *are* an acquition!" cried Gladys, moving from behind Charlie, where she had apparently been watching my behaviour, perhaps from the very beginning, for, once Charlie had begun to fuck me I had no senses to see or hear, and I don't know at what precise moment she and Lucia had returned to the room. She kissed me and petted me, and after a while, addressing Charlie, said :—

"Is she still nipping you, Charlie?"

"I think that was the last," said he.

"Very well. Get off her, then."

"Ah! but Gladys has such an awfully nice quim. Let me enjoy it a little longer."

"Nonsense, boy Get up, I tell you.

It is time we all bathed and dressed for dinner "

" Ah well, I suppose I must But oh, Susan, won't we just have a night of it? Do you like me, dear? "

Oh! I gave him such a kiss, and such a hug and such a sweet little buck, before he began to move, that he swore he never had had such a sweet, darling, responsive girl before in all his life.

" Did I not tell you she was a perfect diamond? " cried Lucia, delighted Charlie slowly, slowly, withdrew his ardent prick, which as it issued sprang up as if it had been suddenly released from something holding it down, but the moment Gladys saw it she cried out —

" Why—oh, my goodness, Charlie! your letter has burst!

And so it had Charlie's prick was entirely through it It was all rucked up about the middle of its shaft

" Jump up, Susan; come with me, cried Gladys; and Lucia, taking me by the arm, pulled me in a way which rather alarmed me.

"Don't be frightened, darling!" said Lucia; "but the sooner we get Charlie's spend out of you the better!"

I felt a great deal of it running out of me then. I could feel it running down my thighs, but the recollection of the tadpoles frightened me a bit, and I ran upstairs, following Gladys as quickly as I could She and Lucia took me into a handsome little boudoir, and through it into a fine bathroom, where they made me tuck up my dress and petticoats, and sit on a small stool covered with American cloth, which felt very cool as I sat down on it. Lucia got a basin and put it between my feet, Gladys brought an enema and a bottle Lucia got a small vessel and water, and in a wonderfully short time I had the tube in me, and a torrent of "safety" liquid was cleaning me from that spend which had been so exquisitely pleasant to feel dashing into me.

Having tenderly wiped me between my thighs the two girls took me back into he boudoir, or as Lucia called it the *Joutour*

It was Gladys s, and oh, so beautiful. Tha it was intended for the offices of love wa instantly apparent. The wall was hung with beautiful pictures, some in oils, some in watercolors, some engravings and some beautifully executed pencil or crayon drawings, but all, whether large or small, were of the most exciting erotic nature. Venus and Adonis, Diana and Endymion, Jupiter and Leda, Jupiter and Danæ and many other mythological love scenes were there, with innumerable others representing amorous couples under almost every conceivable circumstance. Even love in a carriage in Rotten Row was depicted, showing the possibility of a rapturous fuck in the very midst of a crowd. And all were really beautifully painted or drawn, by no means the work of an indifferent artist. A choice collection of erotic literature, some hundred volumes or so of prose and poetry, was in full view in a handsome bookcase. The very letter-weights on the writing-table were erotic—either human couples in the very act, or animals, such as a stallion and mare bull and cow, and so forth Of course there was an ottoman How often I wonder has Gladys given some active lover of hers joy on it.

There we sat and talked for a while until the handsome Annette came and announced that the bath was ready.

Oh, my dear male readers! if you only could have seen the three lovely naked nymphs who bathed their charms in that splendid marble basin; if you could but have seen the equally lovely handmaid, in all her beautiful nudity, plying soap and sponge and towel—I include myself, I know I am well made and pretty—I wonder which one of us would have made your blood boil the hottest and quickest All four of us were dark-haired, and nature had been kind in giving us plenty of glory on our heads and on our mottes too.

Gladys's bush was the blackest Her hair was really black She was most splendidly formed Such shoulders. Such arms Such beautiful breasts and thighs. No wonder men delighted in her. She

...ked **voluptuous** from head to foot, and ... as voluptuous as she looked.

...ucia had taught me what pleasure one ... can give another, but her caresses, ardent as they were, paled before the glory of those which Gladys could give. I learnt much from Lucia, but oh! how much more from my cousin Gladys!

After our bath Lucia introduced me to my own " foutoir " and bedroom. Like Gladys's it was a very handsomely adorned room, with books, pictures, ornaments, and everything of a luxuriously and voluptuously erotic nature. There was the ottoman also, and well did I use it during the next few days. For our lovers soon heard of my arrival, and came running up to town to see and taste their new mistress. The ottoman was the consolatory article of those who could not immediately secure the night with me, or with Gladys, or Lucia ; and came into play almost every afternoon. I have sometimes given delight to four different admirers in the course of two hours, I loved it, but I loved my bed much better.

And what a bed I had never dreamt of one like it It was immense and delicious in every sense It was a four-poster of the most solid mahogany, its posts being of extra strength to support a huge mirror which formed its conopy Mirrors also, slightly inclined inwards, formed three sides of it, so that I could see every movement of my lover, whilst I felt his action and his power And my lover, whilst lying by my side, could see my naked charms in front of him, or as it were suspended over him. So that not only had I the pleasure of being fucked, but I could enjoy seeing myself enjoyed, and, as Lucia said, it was indeed a fetching sight.

We sat down eight to dinner. I was introduced to Allan MacAllan, and the other gentlemen, and although nothing very spicy was allowed in our conversation, we had a very merry party in which the very restrictions placed upon us made our wit all the more poignant By degrees I felt the ants crawling again. Charlie's prick had driven them away, but one fuck is by no means enough, and that a first one too What added still more to the fire which consumed me was a small glass of some very delicate and delicious liqueur, which we all partook of. I contained some powerful aphrodisiac, and I would have been better without it, for I was burning. It took all I knew to prevent me making myself appear what I was randy beyond anything I had ever felt.

But, in Park Lane we, though late sleepers are early bed goers. At ten we said good-night to the gentlemen, and retired to our rooms. Annette came to assist me to undress, and when I was naked she produced my nightdress. What a dress! It was of some exquisitely fine and absolutely transparent silken material. It had no sleeves, but it fastened round my throat with a ribband which ran through eyelet holes. It was open from top to bottom, but fastened just above my breasts by ribbands which were tied, and again below my breasts, across my waist at my hips but so that the ribbands hid none of my bush, and again, but more loosely, at my knees. Its utility as an article of dress was nil, but it greatly added to the attractiveness of my charms by just veiling them.

I had no sooner donned this elegant costume than Charlie appeared, and Annette, wishing us a good-night, went off to prepare for her lover.

Oh Charlie! No! my nightdress might be very fetching, but my naked skin was much more so. The moment he was naked, and he stripped entirely, he untied all my ribbands, and there I was, as naked as himself.

Can I write down all the extravagancies of his behaviour—extravagancies which I, so far from finding outrageous, enjoyed to the uttermost. Ah, dear girls, dear readers believe me, my pen fails me.

What a night we had! What kissing, caressing, fucking! If I had enjoyed what Lucia called No. 1, oh! how I revelled in No. 2! what extra bliss there was in No 3! how superlatively delicious was No. 4! and we did not *end* with *No.* 9, because we began again on waking, and completed No 12! After *that* Charlie acknowledged himself defeated! His proud prick begged for repose, and some time during the day he retreated to the country, having been, as he said, exhausted by the over-enjoyment of the naked charms of his charming cousin,

www.ingramcontent.com/pod-product-compliance
Lightning Source LLC
Chambersburg PA
CBHW080437110426
42743CB00016B/3190